CW00862899

"Julip"

Growing up in Mt. Juliet, Tennessee
Late 1940s Through Early 1960s

by Ron Castleman

outskirts
press

Julip
Growing Up in Small Town America
All Rights Reserved.
Copyright © 2021 Ron Castleman
v4.0

The opinions expressed in this manuscript are solely the opinions of the author and do not represent the opinions or thoughts of the publisher. The author has represented and warranted full ownership and/or legal right to publish all the materials in this book.

This book may not be reproduced, transmitted, or stored in whole or in part by any means, including graphic, electronic, or mechanical without the express written consent of the publisher except in the case of brief quotations embodied in critical articles and reviews.

Outskirts Press, Inc.
http://www.outskirtspress.com

Paperback ISBN: 978-1-9772-3196-3
Hardback ISBN: 978-1-9772-3235-9

Cover Designer: George Rothacker
Cover Art on Back Cover: Evalena Castleman Bennett

Outskirts Press and the "OP" logo are trademarks belonging to Outskirts Press, Inc.

PRINTED IN THE UNITED STATES OF AMERICA

Dedicated in Loving Memory of

My Parents, Macon and Katie

My Brother Richard and my Sister Evalena.

Table of Contents

Introduction

RON CASTLEMAN HAS done us all a great service in writing *"Julip"*. In recording his memories and in clarifying them with careful research, he has given himself "some inner peace," and has given us a wonderful glimpse (a second look for those of us old enough to remember) into those important years in the late 1940s and early 1960s in Mt. Juliet.

The facts are here. In relating his father's and brother's experiences as highly skilled craftsmen of many talents, Ron shows us what it was like to start, manage, and maintain a business before, during, and after World War II. The pictures illustrate his points in supporting ways that words could never do.

We learn about the challenges of constructing a blockhouse while living in the garage-home underneath. And, as interesting as the building is, the implied story of the family's obvious determination to maintain their love and respect for each other is even more impressive.

Two chapters, "Scrapbook of Nine Fiery Years" and "The Fire Chief" are important local history and beg for reprinting to a wider audience. Using pictures and newspaper article reprints, Ron has illuminated an era in Mt. Juliet's history that has never, to my knowledge, been so thoroughly covered. Particularly, "Scrapbook of Nine Fiery Years" instantly becomes the definitive history of those incredible years when it must have seemed that the very gates of Hell had been opened on the village. The chronological retelling of those times by reprinting the words of those who were reporting events as they happened is a credit to Ron's lack of ego and his concern for historical accuracy.

In addition to the facts, the supporting pictures, newspaper articles, and other items of research lend credibility to the chapters that personal reminiscences alone could not accomplish. These items will cause you to keep returning to *"Julip"* through the years to remind yourself of when the events occurred and to settle arguments with relatives and friends when your own memories of those times cannot be reconciled.

The feelings are here. As valuable as the local history is in these pages (and it is of considerable value), the very spirit of the book taps into more universal feelings we all recognize and experience.

Ron's journey through "Small Town America" in Chapter One, with one loving detail piled on top of another and another, gives us a sense of place that is as comforting as a mother's arms. It's no accident that the comparison is made to "It's A Wonderful Life."

Read the "Background" of Chapter 7, "First Call to Breakfast," and ask yourself if this short chapter is just about making biscuits…I don't think so. Katie Castleman may have been "the family's alarm clock'" but, if you read between the lines here and throughout the book, you may decide that she provided the love and nurture that helped to bond the family ties so strongly.

The entire saga of Castleman's Garage, as related here, is a testimony of family pride, mutual support, and loving tolerance. The times change from horseback to horsepower; the culture evolves through radio, movies, and television; yet, the thread that runs so true, undergirding all, is the family.

If you weren't in Mt. Juliet in those years, then your reading of *"Julip"* may remind you of places in your heart that are special and will always be with you. If you were there, then you will have your own memories of Castleman's Garage. It was a place where the Castleman family waited on you, repaired your automobile, sold you an appliance, or helped you with some special problem. But, for some people, it has become much more. The memories of Castleman's Garage, mixed with our feelings in looking back to those times, makes it a sacred place, a focal point around which we write our own version of *"Julip"* in our minds. For that, we can be grateful to Ron Castleman for the writing of *"Julip"* and for its reminders of the importance of things past.

Charles Lee McCorkle

Preface

THIS BOOK ACTUALLY began in 1978 on an airplane somewhere between Los Angeles and New York City. I've gotten some of my best inspirations and perspectives at 37,000 feet. My first effort, "The Fire Chief" (now Chapter 6), was written as a birthday gift for my Dad on his 68th birthday in November of 1978. My next writing, "Mother and Ladies' Night at the Men's Club" (Chapter 13) was written for Mother as a Christmas gift in 1979.

Seventeen years passed before I was inspired to write again. In late 1997 I wrote a few more chapters and combined them with the first two to create a simple manuscript called *"Julip"*. I gave each member of my family a copy for Christmas that year. A few more copies were given to carefully selected Mt. Juliet friends whom I thought might have an appreciation for it and who wouldn't grade my work too hard.

The 1997 effort gave me the self-confidence I needed to continue *"Julip"* as a work in progress. I wrote more chapters and finished the second edition in 1998. I once again gave family members copies for Christmas. Distribution to folks in Mt. Juliet, my extended family, doubled from the year before.

I intended to finish the third and final edition of *"Julip"* by the end of 1999. A few days before Christmas of that year I reluctantly accepted it was an unrealistic goal. It was one time in my life when I followed my heart and didn't let a deadline (albeit self-imposed) rule my behavior.

The delay resulted in the 1999-2000 edition, which expanded the work to 14 chapters and included an "Introduction" by Charles Lee McCorkle, my life-long close friend who shares my love for Mt. Juliet. He was a co-witness to most of what I've written and encouraged me to keep writing about those special times.

One of the most rewarding parts of writing this book was looking up old friends ...many of whom I hadn't seen in over 30 years. Even though so much time had passed each person extended a warm Mt. Juliet welcome and I felt a loving connection. They each helped with memories and facts I could use in conjunction with old newspaper articles, school yearbooks, The Mt. Juliet Library and other reliable sources.

For me, recalling experiences from the past is unpredictable. Some days nothing at all comes to mind; other days I'll recall a fragment or two. Then occasionally I have a day where memories flood my mind. I'm beginning to get better at writing them down before they are forgotten. Writing about memory flow reminds me of a little sign my Dad had hanging in Castleman's Garage for many years that read, "Business flows like a ketchup bottle, first none il' come, then a lott'l". Substitute the word memories for business and that's me.

I attribute a major part of any small measure of success I may have achieved in life to my wonderful family and to all my Mt. Juliet friends......my extended family. The good fortune I had of growing up in a small town is priceless and something of which I am very proud.

Writing *"Julip"* has been one of the most enjoyable chapters in my life. I wanted to permanently record what happened, because the stories I've tried to relay are *too important to be forgotten*.

Twenty years have passed and it's now November of 2020 but none of the memories or facts have changed. The last eight months of time stuck at home during the Corona Virus pandemic enabled me to finish polishing my manuscript, add a fifteenth chapter I wrote three years ago, and finally publish *"Julip"*.

CHAPTER 1

Small Town America

IN 1950 MT. Juliet was a very small rural Tennessee town. Located smack dab in the middle of the state, it was small...but on the map. The World Book Encyclopedias our family purchased in 1951 showed the results of the 1950 U.S. Census with Mt. Juliet reporting a population of 706.

Rather than a town, Mt. Juliet was actually more of a quiet village surrounded by homes, farms and lush rolling hills. Most of the families who didn't own farms had ample land for a large vegetable garden and at least a few chickens.

It was a great time to grow up in small town America. I was privileged to have been born into an extraordinary family and to have lived in an extraordinary town. I felt a sense of being valued, not just within my family, but by most everyone in town. If you were a kid who lived in or near the village of Mt. Juliet in 1950 you were probably like me.... happy.

I had the secure feeling I could wander most anywhere in town and if needed I could ask anyone for help. I assumed everyone knew who I was. In the highly unlikely event, they didn't know me I could simply tell them I was Macon and Katie's boy and everything would be okay.

Crime was almost non-existent. Even though there were no streetlights it was safe to walk home after dark and no one locked their doors. While there was no police department or sheriff, we had something even better. Buell Agee, who lived right in the heart of Mt. Juliet, was our local Constable and could be counted on to keep things peaceful (as far as I know he never failed to be reelected).

To say the town was friendly and that everyone was known on a first name basis was an understatement. To be accurate, very few people were actually called by their first name. Instead there was an even friendlier name system.

Many people were called only by their nicknames. Two of my favorites were "Mush" Agee and "Possum" Bates. It was years before I knew that "Mush's" real name was Nealon and "Possum's" real name was Calvin. I do know that "Possum" had a passion for possum hunting, but I still don't know how Nealon earned the nickname "Mush".

Others were always called by their first <u>and</u> middle names. For example, Charles Lee McCorkle was always called "Charles Lee" and I never heard anyone call him just Charles.

Some folks were referred to only by their first two initials. I'm sure "Z. I." Brewer had a first and middle name, and even though I knew him and his family well, I still don't know his real name.

A couple of people were called by their real names, but they were so unusual I thought they were nicknames.

Over the years I've compiled quite a list of those friendly monikers.

Nicknames	Called by Both Their First <u>and</u> Middle Names, etc.	Called by First and <u>Middle</u> Initials	Unusual Names
"Beans" Griffin	"Annie Kate" James	"A. D." Martin, Jr.	Dempsey
"Booty" Cummings	"Miss Annie Lou"	"A. N." Robinson	Curry
"Boots" Searcy	McDaniel	"A. R." Tomlinson	Glespie Smith
"Brigger" Pike	"Bennie Frank" Wilson	"A. T." Duke	Grills Foster
"Brownie"	"Benny Lee" Sperry	"C. B." Smith	Oco Hamblen
Robinson	"Betty Joyce" Agee	"C. G." Yelton	Wurt Paty
"Butch" Page	"Bobbie Jean" Moore	"C. J." Potter	
"Buzzy" Rice	"Carl Douglas"	"E. D." James	
"Cabbage Head"	Prentice	"J. R." Lawson	
Sutherland	"Charles Lee"	"N. C." Hibbett	
"Chick" Lowe	McCorkle	"O. F. Howell"	
"Chip" Sharp	"Charles Shannon"	"R. B." James	
"Coochie" Graves	Everett	"W. C." Smith	

"Corn" Butler
"Dick" Castleman
"Diddy" McCulloch
"Doc" Smith
"Dude" Hibbett
"Fat" Hackney
"Fergie" Ferguson
"Fuzzy" Ozment
"Goober" Eakes
"Grease" Castleman
"Hooty" Smith
"Hump" McCorkle
"Jockey" Yelton
"Little Bit"
McCulloch
"Mãc" (Mãcon)
Castleman
"Mãter" Bates
"Money Bags" Page
"Muggs" McKee
"Mush" Agee
"Nabe" McCulloch
"P.D." McCulloch
"Pie Face" aka "P
Pup" Petty
"Pinky" Quarles
"Pop" Smartt
"Possum" Bates
"Preacher"
Cawthon
"Rass" Poindexter
"Roughhouse"
Smith
"Runt" Hewgley
"Sonny" Hardaway
"Sonny" Potter
"Soup" Donnell
"Spider" Stewart
"Termite"
McCullough
"Toe Joe" Petty
"Toppie" McFarland
"Two" Smith

"Della Mae" Agee
"Earl Wayne"
McCulloch
"Edward Allen"
Green
"Guy Gene" Yelton
"James Lester" Eakes
"Homer Dean"
Tomlinson
"Howard Junior"
Young
"Hugh B." James
"Iva Nell" Smith
"James Noel" Hayes
"James Robert" Eakes
"John Bell" Viverett
"John Wayne"
Everette
"Mary Alfred"
Hackney
"Mary Helen" Bass
"Mary Lawton"
Lasater
"Mary Margaret"
Smith
"Mary Poe" Williams
"May Eunice" Falkner
"Minnie Jo"
Derryberry
"Norma Kay" Smith
"Paul Wilson" Swain
"Percy Carver" Young
"Robert Wayne"
Ashley
"Rose Marie" Begarly
"Ruby Lou" Bates
"Ruby Pearl" Foster
"Willie B." Jennings

"W. T." Bates
"Z. I." Brewer
"Z.O." Matthews

Even Mt. Juliet had a nickname...to some of us it was affection-
ately known as *"Julip"*.

The streets and roads, many of which were unpaved, had no formal
names. The railroad track, which ran east and west through the center of town, was often used as a reference point for giving directions.
Several times each day, a train from the Tennessee Central Railroad
would stop to unload and load passengers, mail or other parcels. The
Tennessee Central offered no train depot but did provide a small three
wall shelter with the name "**MT. JULIET**" on each end. If you were
standing at the shelter waiting for a train you could look to the west
and see a white vertical marker with the number 17 which was a reminder to the train engineer that Nashville was 17 miles away.

Shortly before the train came through town on its morning and
afternoon schedules, an elderly gentleman by the name of Sam Bond
would go to a shed attached to the U.S. Post office and retrieve a
red pushcart with large buggy wheels. From there he would push
the cart to an elevated delivery door and Mrs. Vesta Locke, the local
Postmistress, would hand mail sacks down to him. He then slowly
rolled the cart about 75 yards to the train track and waited for its arrival. When the train stopped, men from the mail car would exchange
mail sacks and packages with Mr. Bond. He would then return the
filled cart to the post office.

I would often follow along and watch as he went about his duties
and I became familiar with the entire process. Frequently I would race
ahead of him and be inside the Post Office when he arrived. Because I
knew Mrs. Locke and Mrs. Nancy Hackney, her sister who also worked
at the Post Office, I could always talk my way beyond the area where
the public was allowed and be on the interior side of the elevated door
by the time Mr. Bond would pitch the mail sacks up from his cart. I
learned how to open the drawstring on the large canvas mail sacks and
dump the mail on the floor for sorting. I'm sure it was against the rules

for me to do this but remember this was a small town.

Mt. Juliet's entire business district was about one city block in size. Starting on the north side of the railroad track was the Bank of Mt. Juliet, which was known as the oldest bank in Wilson County. As you entered the bank you always received a friendly greeting from Miss Estelle at the left teller's window (Mrs. Estelle Evins) and Miss Annie Lou at the right window (Mrs. Annie Lou McDaniel). Both ladies were kind, friendly and compassionate to everyone...much like George Bailey (played by Jimmy Stewart) who ran the Bedford Falls Building and Loan in the movie, *"It's a Wonderful Life"*.

The second floor of the bank was home for the Harvey Freeman Chapter of the Eastern Star and The Mt. Juliet Masonic Lodge. Because my Mother and Father were active in each respectively for a number of years, we occasionally got to visit this intriguing part of the building when meetings were not in progress. Part of the visit's intrigue was getting there via the black metal exterior stairway located at the rear of the building. Its resemblance to a fire escape was a climbing attraction children couldn't resist.

Next door to the bank building, and separated only by a narrow alley, was Young's Grocery, which was run by Howard and Louise Young. At Young's you could get an ice cream cone with either vanilla, chocolate, strawberry or fudge ripple, or check out a book made possible through the Wilson County Bookmobile.

Young's was one of four grocery stores in Mt. Juliet. The other three were on the south side of the tracks, which meant all four were within a quarter mile of each other.

In addition to selling groceries they all had many other things in common; they were all places where people gathered to visit one another; the owners knew everyone by their first name and sold groceries on credit; they all sold feed, seeds, nails, kerosene, stove pipe, coal scuttles, etc. …and all had screen doors at the entrance with the following words stenciled in yellow paint across the screen wire:

Just outside the front door of each store was a large yellow wooden breadbox where the Colonial Bread deliveryman from Nashville deposited loaves of fresh bread before sunup each morning. As each store opened, the fresh bread was moved inside the store to the bread rack.

One other thing common to each was the ability to have the proprietor make you a sandwich back at the meat cooler. It was really like a deli of today, but deli wasn't yet in our vocabulary. Sandwiches were made to order by removing a large piece of ham or bologna from the meat cooler and placing it on the electric meat slicer. As the meat was sliced it was placed on a fresh piece of white butcher's paper where it was assembled with "light" (white) bread for a sandwich. There was no place to eat the sandwich so you either ate it standing up or carried it with you.

Once you left Young's and headed south across the railroad tracks there was a one-story white stucco building on the right that housed four small businesses. First was Joe Hunt's Barbershop where I got my first haircut. It fascinated me to watch the scissors in Mr. Hunt's right hand. He would make a slow careful cut of hair with the scissors and then as he moved them away from the hair his hand would make the scissors open and close hundreds of times in the air before slowing for the next cut. Mr. Hunt's was one of the few barbershops where I actually saw someone get a shave or use a spittoon. Next, and in the same suite, were Yelton's & Taylors Insurance and Real Estate Office and Mrs. Irene Yelton's Dress Shop. Last but not least in the third suite was Les Force's Shoe Repair Shop where I first became familiar with "Cat's Paw" brand of replacement shoe heels.

Directly across the street was A. R. Tomlinson's Store. In addition to groceries, Mr. Tomlinson also sold Mobil Gasoline and entertained customers with lots of conversation.

Immediately adjacent to Tomlinson's were Smith's Store and The Frozen Food Bank, both of which were contained in one large building. C.B. Smith's Store, which was the most up-to-date grocery store in Mt. Juliet, took up about two-thirds of the building. In addition to groceries, one long wall of the store was set aside for the sale of shoes, rubber boots, overshoes, various items of clothing, cloth and sewing accessories.

The remaining third of the building was The Frozen Food Bank, which was operated by Mildred McCorkle, C.B. Smith's daughter. Most of the time I heard people refer to The Frozen Food Bank as simply "The Locker". In addition to being a frozen food bank, it was also a meat-processing center, hardware store and bait & tackle shop. A large sliding door was usually open so customers could easily flow from one business to the other.

McCorkle's food locker was a fun place to visit. It was built before people had deep freezes to preserve their harvests of beef, pork, poultry or vegetables. If you rented a food locker you were given a key to secure your items. You could access your locker, anytime during store hours, by opening an extremely heavy and thick door and entering a large room where the temperature was maintained below freezing around the clock. From the same cold room, blocks of ice were available for purchase for old-fashioned electric ice boxes, to feed an ice cream churn or to ice down cold drinks (soft drinks) for a family reunion or a church gathering that was followed by "dinner on the grounds".

At the rear of the Smith and McCorkle building was the source of the live fishing bait sold at McCorkle's...a worm ranch where beds of fishing worms were raised for sale.

Across the street from Smith's and McCorkle's was Toppie's. Toppie's, which was owned and operated by Toppie McFarland, was our local soda fountain and the closest thing we had to a drug store. Out in front he sold Sinclair gasoline and in an adjacent building, Ferguson farm tractors and implements. My Dad referred to this adjacent green building, which sat just to the north of Toppie's, as the "Green Shop". Prior to WWII, he had rented it from Toppie for several years as the location for Castleman Auto Repair.

Toppie's was a place where students could go after school and listen to songs on a Wurlitzer Jukebox. Many hours were spent there sipping a milkshake or fountain coke on one of the counter stools or eating a burger in one of the booths.

Right behind Toppie's was an old blacksmith shop, which had long since ceased operation and was being used only as a storage building. Next to it was a saloon that was no longer open and in a state of decay. Both the blacksmith shop and saloon looked like they were right out of a western movie.

The fourth and last grocery store in town was Jordan's (pronounced Jerdan's) which was part of the same structure as the Post Office. While I'm sure all of the grocery stores sold them, I specifically remember Jordan's selling the perfect bottled soft drink for children; "Grapette" had the taste of a NeHi Grape soft drink but came in a small bottle, about half the size of a 6 ounce bottle of CocaCola. Jordan's also sold small round cups of ice cream. The neat thing was not just using a small wooden spoon to eat the ice cream but also finding a movie star's picture under the round lid.

Next to Jordan's was a large building that was at one time the Mt.

Juliet depot for the N.C. & Saint L. Railroad (Nashville, Chattanooga and St. Louis). The N.C. & Saint L. tracks had been removed years before and the "Old Railroad Bed", as it was called, became one of the main roads for automobile traffic. The old depot building had been converted into the local telephone office by the Mt. Juliet Telephone Company. To make a phone call you simply picked up the phone and waited for an operator to say, "number please". If you were calling our home, you'd say "881-W please"; if you wanted to reach my Dad at work you'd say "321 please". If you were lazy you could ask for the party by name, but it wasn't encouraged. In 1950 the phone company was owned by Walter Phillips, but a year or two later he sold it to Ernest and Fontelle Sutherland. The Sutherlands and their children lived in part of the depot.

The Mt. Juliet Post Office was located across from the telephone office. The post office was the building nearest Castleman's Garage - my Dad's place.

Located right in the middle of Mt. Juliet's business district was an empty grassy lot that was Mt. Juliet's village green. Since all of the businesses surrounded it, it became a well-traversed connecting point. A footpath ran east to west from Mt. Juliet Road to the post office, Jordan's Store and other destinations. Folks would often stop to chat and visit along this path. Midway on the path was the town's public re-stroom, an outdoor toilet. On more than one Halloween it was moved from that location. On one occasion some overzealous boys used it for a bonfire at the town's crossroad (Mt. Juliet Road and The Old Railroad Bed). Somehow their identity was eventually determined, and I was part of the audience that watched them build a new one.

On an earlier occasion the village green was the location for a July 4th Barbeque fundraiser by the Mt. Juliet Masonic Lodge. A long pit was dug east to west and covered with fence wire so the pork barbecue could cook all night and be ready to sell by lunchtime on the 4th. I can still smell it cooking.

For a while on Saturday evenings I watched an enterprising out-of-towner drive his large truck on to the lot. On the back of the truck was a movie projector, which he used to show movies on the white rear wall of Yelton's and Taylor's Real Estate and Insurance Office. After paying a small admission charge, folks would watch the movie (usually a cartoon and a western) while sitting on the wooden benches he provided or on the front fenders of their cars.

The lot was also used for Gospel tent meetings, impromptu football and baseball games, bicycle knock out races and an occasional scuffle.

If I wasn't an active participant in the village green activities, I at least always had a front row seat a few feet away while working at Castleman's Garage. If I was supposed to be helping my Dad and there was a football or baseball game going on, I was in agony because I couldn't be part of the game. As I got older, it was my duty to handle all the gasoline customers after school. Many times, I would sneak over and play in the game when I shouldn't have. When a gasoline customer would drive across the driveway signal bell everyone got used to the game going into a timeout while I ran over to pump gas. More about Castleman's Garage in the next chapter.

Smith's Grocery circa 1945. The grocery was on the left and the Frozen Food Bank, "The Locker", was on the right. The locker was yet to be painted as a result of the recent construction to add it on to the store. Mr. C.B.'s Buick sits to the left of the building. On the sidewalk under the left awning a grocery delivery bicycle awaits the next customer. To the right of the bicycle is one of the Colonial Bread Company's yellow breadboxes. The slanted top of this breadbox was a favorite perch at any hour of the day for viewing the local action or holding court with others who gathered just to talk. (Many people who lived in Mt. Juliet during this era have fond memories of their time from one of the best seats in the Mt. Juliet). The small boy and girl standing in front of the store are from the left, Charles Lee McCorkle and Linda McCorkle. Smith's Store later became known as Smith and McCorkle's and finally just McCorkles. (Photo courtesy of Charles Lee McCorkle).

Mt. Juliet as it looked in 1947 and the way I remember it looking until at least 1955. Seated: from the left is Truman Hibbett, Bobby "Corn" Butler and N. C. Hibbett, Jr. Standing: from the left is Kenneth Donnell, Richard Castleman, Jerry Hackney and Jimmy Butler.

1. Jordan's Grocery Store; 2. Bank of Mt. Juliet, Masonic Lodge Hall and Young's Grocery Store; 3. Old Saloon; 4. Willis' Blacksmith Shop; 5. A. R. Tomlinson's Grocery Store and Gas Station; 6. Toppie's.
7. Smith's Grocery Store and Frozen Food Bank. (Photo courtesy of N.C. Hibbett, Jr.)

Home of the Mt. Juliet Post Office from the early 1940s through the early 1960s. That's me trudging throuh a foot of snow to Castleman's Garage which was next door. More on Castleman's Garage in the next chapter. Photo c. 1960

CHAPTER 2

Castleman's Garage

MOST EVERYONE I knew thought my Dad, Macon Castleman, was the best auto mechanic anywhere. He was self-taught and could repair just about anything mechanical or electrical. He was also great at diagnosing the real source of a mechanical or electrical problem. His diagnostic skills always saved customers money by avoiding the trial and error approach of bolting on expensive parts they didn't need. In addition to the excellent quality of his work, he was known for his dependability, honesty, fairness and hard work. He was a pillar of the community.

The whole family helped in the business. My three sisters, Evalena, Janice and Bettye, helped by sweeping the garage floor. My brother Richard and I each spent our first twenty years in life working for our Dad as apprentice mechanics before moving on to our own careers. Our Mom kept the books, drove cars and trucks in connection with road service and kept the peace (in addition to her other full-time job as a Mother of 5). Within the family we referred to Castleman's Garage as either the "garage" or the "shop".

To heat the shop Daddy bought a potbelly stove from war surplus, which I understand was used in an Army barrack. On cold mornings we would freeze until the fire was going. Daddy always started the fire the same way. First, he would cut a few sticks of small kindling with a hatchet; next he would tear part of a cardboard box in strips and lay it over the kindling. On top of the cardboard went a large shovel full of coal. Finally, he would pitch about a fourth of a pint of gasoline on top of the coal, quickly strike a match on the side of the stove and throw it in. I was taught to always stand beside the stove when the match was thrown in and never in front, at its opening, just in case you put in a little too much gasoline. I can still hear the scary "whoomp" sound of the gasoline igniting. As you might imagine, this method of starting a fire was always successful but as they say, don't try this at home. It's rather ironic that Mt. Juliet established a volunteer fire department in 1950, and, despite this unorthodox method of starting a fire, Daddy became it's first fire chief!

Some folks stood next to the stove while my Dad repaired their cars while others would just come by to loaf and visit with others. On very cold days the shop was extremely hard to heat and the only warm area was right around the stove. We would get the fire going so big and hot the cast iron stove had a red glow. You had to keep turning your body to keep from freezing on one side and roasting on the other.

I heard many great stories being told by friendly town folks while hugging that potbelly stove. Its warmth was a focal point that brought out the best of people and encouraged our sense of community.

It is funny how you remember only the best parts of those good old days and forget what it was like to go out in the cold to bring in more coal or carry out the ashes. Still...what I wouldn't give to hug that old potbelly just one more time!

That Man and Machine Feeling

"Okay", Daddy called out from the mechanics creeper underneath the car, "that's the last bolt...give it a try". Richard used both hands to pull downward on the long chain from the hoist that hung from the huge steel beam some 20 feet above. The first tug didn't change things much. Then with another pull you knew something big was about to happen. By this time Daddy was standing near Richard and me peering down into the engine compartment of a '48 Ford.

Hours earlier the car had been carefully positioned in that special bay at the front of the garage which was reserved for long term projects like engine swaps or other big overhaul jobs. On this occasion we were removing the engine so Daddy could completely rebuild it.

First the car's hood had been removed to allow plenty of elbowroom and access from the big chain hoist above. The radiator was removed next so the engine could swing forward as it was uncoupled from the transmission and then lifted from the car. All sorts of other parts were removed and placed in the car's trunk or an out of the way space on the concrete floor. This included all the screws, nuts, bolts, brackets, covers, fan belts and a variety of other items that make a car go. The electrical wiring and fuel lines had been disconnected and carefully moved out of the way. The all-important bolts from the engines two front motor mounts had been removed. Finally, the 6 to 8 large bolts that fasten the transmission to the engine had been given their last counter clockwise turn with a 5/8" box-end wrench…the final few turns were coaxed by the grip of Daddy's thumb and forefinger.

You could tell the weight of the engine was still resting on the frame of the car, but the hoist's chain had gone from a flexible "at ease state" to a tense and stressed "ATTENTION". Daddy nodded to Richard to make one more pull on the chain and the engine wiggled a little. Now Daddy was reaching down with both hands on the engine to wiggle it in a side to side and forward motion away from the transmission. Richard sensed another pull on the chain was needed and did so without being asked. The engine began to move forward and upward as it finally slid free from the transmission. The front fenders on the Ford began to rise upward with each additional pull of the chain. Another pull, then another and another. Things were really beginning to happen. Now the engine was dangling and only touching the engine compartment here and there. No longer was it being cradled in the car's frame. Next came the big moment which always had the same climactic feeling. The engine was hoisted straight up and completely out of the car. The front of the car was now a good 4 or 5 inches higher and almost appeared to beg for the return of its flathead

V-8 power plant, which now dangled and swayed out of its reach on the chain hoist above.

The mammoth sized garage door behind the Ford was opened and the three of us easily pushed it backward away from the engine until there was nothing but empty space between it and the concrete floor below. A big iron top table was then rolled underneath the engine. By pulling on the opposite chain the hoist lowered its heavy catch down to the table below. When the chain finally relaxed its tension, the engine rested on its side and was ready for overhaul. At a minimum this would include grinding the valves, replacing the piston rings and crankshaft bearings – a world of precision and tolerances to the thousandth of an inch.

Daddy was a natural born master mechanic. He wasn't a bragging man but he took great pride in telling only me and Richard that after taking an engine completely apart, rebuilding it and then reassembling it he could set the timing, prime the carburetor and start the engine on the first revolution of the starter. This was something only those with the highest of skills could achieve. On more than one occasion I remember local "shade-tree" mechanics attempting engine overhaul work and never being able to start the engine. Even towing the car at 20 miles per hour and then shifting into gear failed. Finally, they would tow the car to Daddy and ask for him to clean up their mess. He never took advantage of people in this embarrassing predicament nor did he make people feel badly about not having him do the work to begin with.

While much of the above was hard physical work, these are all good memories…especially those moments when that big chain hoist lifted an engine out of a car. It never ceased to captivate, excite and satisfy me. I guess it's "that man and machine feeling" that started with me when I played with my first toy cars and trucks. That's one of the feelings that goes back about as far as I can remember.

Richard's Projects

Richard and I learned from Daddy everything we would know about automobiles and anything else mechanical. The three of us had a special bond via our work at the garage and special projects that related to the automotive repair business.

Richard's mechanical projects started at an early age. These projects always included Daddy's interest, encouragement, helping hands and especially his teaching. Daddy taught us that you teach by telling and showing someone how to do something, then step back and watch them try it. He knew if he jumped in and took over in the middle of a failure that we would never learn for ourselves. He also knew when to push if one of us was stuck and didn't know what to do next. If he thought we could figure it out if we just tried, he'd say "get started and do something even if it's wrong".

In the early fifties, when Richard was in his mid-teens, he purchased his first motorcycle from Jim Skulley (at that time around Mt. Juliet, the word motorcycle was pronounced motorsicle...sicle as in popsicle). I remember tagging along with Richard and Daddy to Mr. Skulley's to purchase what had once been a late 20's model Harley Davidson. Several boxes containing numerous engine parts along with two wheels, fenders and a frame were removed from an outbuilding and loaded in the back of our Model-A Ford pick-up truck.

It wasn't long until Richard had not only rebuilt the Harley's engine, but he also sanded and painted every square inch of the frame, fenders, etc. The end product was a dazzling like-new motorcycle in a beautiful dark green color. He later sold this Harley to George Page but continued to own progressively newer and better Harley's throughout his teenage years. He was a skillful rider and could really handle a Harley.

In about 1954 he started his next project...a worn out 1948 Ford Convertible with no top and a bad engine. His restoration from the inside out included a new black paint job, a new top and new upholstery. He rebuilt the Ford's original flathead V-8 engine, spray painted it and then with a small horsehair brush he proudly printed the following across each cylinder head: *"Completely Rebuilt by Castleman's Garage"*.

He later became dissatisfied with the car's original engine and replaced it with an overhead valve V-8 from a wrecked 1950 Oldsmobile. This was quite an engineering feat that required many modifications to the car and a special adapter plate to marry the Olds engine to the Ford Transmission. This was one project Richard could not do by himself. Daddy's years of experience and inventiveness were essential throughout the project. I remember the fabrication of custom-made front motor mounts that he designed and welded together from various metals.

Richard's "Fordmobile", as he called it, was truly his pride and joy.

Innovation and Creativity

Daddy was faced with auto repair challenges daily. The method that worked one day would not necessarily work the next. Nothing was routine. It could be the same model car, a similar complaint but a different owner. If the owner had neglected or abused the car the challenge seemed to be greater than if the car had received tender loving care. He admired anyone who took good care of their automobile and he was not afraid to let a neglectful customer know what they could do better.

Daddy's gifts were patience, high intelligence, a great capacity to learn on his own and the ability to analyze a problem so a quick non-circuitous solution could be found. If removing a nut or bolt was difficult, brute force was never an option. There was always a more skillful method that used less physical energy and caused the least amount of damage to surrounding parts. This in turn saved the customer money.

In addition to the skill set listed above was his ability to innovate and be creative. While much of this came out of necessity, I think these traits were enhanced by listening to classical music while he worked. He had a turntable, amplifier and large speakers at the garage. His vinyl LP collection enabled him to hear favorite pieces performed by symphonic orchestras from around the country. I do not know of any other auto shop where they played classical music. Our customers did not seem to mind at all. During the day, the music was often drowned out by a passing train or the everyday sounds heard in an auto repair shop. So, he mostly enjoyed the music when no one was around or late at night. It was during this quiet time alone that he did his best thinking and became his most creative.

One of dozens of examples I can think of regarding innovation and creativity involved automatic transmissions. By the late 1950s more and more cars hit the market with automatic transmissions instead of standard. For example, Ford offered the Ford-O-Matic, Chevrolet the PowerGlide, Buick the Dynaflow, etc. Manufacturers were still finding their groove for long term reliability, so this created an expanded opportunity for repair work.

My Dad was always trying to stay current with the market, so he studied books and began teaching himself how to rebuild automatic transmissions using a 1952 Ford as a guinea pig.

The automatic transmission is an extremely complex mechanism and a complete departure from anything he had learned in the past. The challenge involved hydraulics, torque converters, regulators, oil pumps, planetary gears, valve bodies and many precision moving parts with tolerances too small to discern by the naked eye.

Most mechanics received factory training or went to technical school to learn this specialty. He was undaunted by the steep learning curve. He became successful as a result of perseverance and his capacity to learn.

Not only did he teach himself this new line of his business, he also designed and built the transmission hoist shown later in the picture section of this chapter. An automatic transmission weighed well over 200 pounds. The hoist enabled him to remove or install a transmission by himself from the underside of the car when it was six feet in the air on our large hydraulic lift.

The transmission was attached with special adapters at the end of a large boom which could be raised or lowered to the desired height by a small hydraulic jack (at the left in the photo). But he also needed to make finite adjustments to the orientation of the transmission. For this he designed a mechanism which enabled him to tilt the rear of the transmission up or down to the angle needed for its tricky removal and reinstallation.

The hoist had to have superior strength to support the heavy weight of a transmission. Some of the various metals he used in making the hoist were parts of an automobile. For example, the base was made from old automobile drive shafts and the wheels were auto wheel bearings.

Once the transmission had been removed from a car the hoist could be rolled to a workbench where it could be offloaded for rebuilding. He attempted but was unsuccessful in getting an automobile trade journal to do a story on how other mechanics could cheaply build a hoist like his.

So, there's another attribute... he was always willing to share his knowledge to anyone who earnestly wanted to learn! *More about this in Chapter 15 near the end of this book.*

Mother and Castleman's Garage

I'd be remiss if I closed this chapter without a greater mention of Mother's significant, but overshadowed, contribution to the success of the family business. Miss Katie, as she was called by everyone outside the family, was personable and well liked by all.

I briefly mentioned her multiple jobs at the beginning of this chapter, but I want to expand on that a bit. She was sort of like the act we used to see in early television on variety shows like Ed Sullivan. Mother is really the one who kept all the plates spinning.

First, she got everyone up in the mornings, cooked a full breakfast, prepared lunches and made plans for a full dinner.

Then there was work at the garage a few hours each day. She did all the record keeping and sent out monthly statements to customers who charged their repair work or gasoline (which was most of them). She greeted customers, took care of banking, went to Lebanon to pick up auto parts orders and even pumped gasoline when one of us was too busy with garage work. At times she would have her sewing machine in the office at the garage so she could continue making garments for people in town to make extra money for the family. There were never any vacations or any other down time for her or my Dad.

In later chapters I write about how she also worked part-time at the medical clinic located in the garage at our home and how she and my three sisters served dinner there to the Mt. Juliet Men's Club every Tuesday night for several years.

All of this was in addition to doing more than half of the parenting and nurturing of her five children because my Dad was always tied up with a 70+ hour workweek. Along with the many hats she wore, it was my Mom's untiring strength that was an essential part of keeping Castleman's Garage going.

Long after Richard had left home and the family business was down to my Dad, Mom and me (after school, on Saturdays and all summer) I recall those times late in the day at the garage where only the three of us were present. The stress of our customers auto repair deadlines and making ends meet while running a family business took its toll. I can still hear her soothing voice of reason pulling us all up and encouraging us through those moments.

A few minutes later she would be off for home to make a delicious dinner for the family while my Dad and I began to close up the shop for the day.

Castleman's Garage, "The Shop", (sometime around 1952 or 1953) and soon after Daddy added gas pumps to begin selling Gulf Gasoline; white exterior paint would come next. Gas sold for about 25 cents a gallon and there were no credit cards...customers would either pay cash or shout "put it on my account" as they drove away. No one had to pump their own gas (self-service gas stations had not been born). Each customer automatically got his or her windshield cleaned, and no one left without being asked "Can I check under the hood for you?"

A short time after the gas pumps were added the concrete block garage build-ing received its first ever coat of white paint. Also, a large sign with simply "Castleman's" was added above the tall office door. (This sign now proudly hangs high on an inside wall of the garage at my home).

I can still hear the sounds the doors made when they were opened, the racks when they went up or down, the bell that rang each time one of the gas pumps delivered another gallon of gas, etc.

Note the Tennessee Central Section house in the background on the far right. (Photo June 1957)

On the left is the old, cast-iron, "Potbelly" stove, which finally cracked from too many "red-hot" fires.

At the top center of the photo you can see the left rear wheel of a car dangling free from what we called the little rack. The wooden workbench and large vise near the center of the photo had quite a history that I unfortunately failed to record when Daddy told me the story. I do remember it had been used in all the previous shops he rented before building a place of his own. Fortunately, the vise got passed on to me.

To the right of the vise are hoses and vertical tanks for his acetylene-oxygen welder (he was particularly good at welding and people in town were often dependent upon him for their welding needs as well as auto repair). The large horizontal tank to the right of the welding equipment supplied compressed air for the two hydraulic lifts, etc. This big noisy air compressor would start at any time; if you happened to be on the phone when this happened, and at the same time you became blessed with the passing of a Tennessee Central train (the tracks were about 100 feet from the shop), all you could do was wait.

A view from the customer area looking toward the work area. A Renault 4CV Daddy was rebuilding is about halfway up on the big rack (hydraulic lift).

A close look at the "Co-Cola" machine, as it was called, reveals a recent price increase from a nickel to six cents. The mechanism that received the nickel was not retrofitted by Coke to receive the extra penny. Instead a small vertical cylinder with a slot in the top was added between the chrome door on the left and the handle in the center. The penny was collected on the honor system. Some customers complained about the extra cost. Since the machine would still dispense Cokes for only a nickel, we were convinced some folks simply thumped the penny canister to make it sound like they put in the penny. Honest, I'm not making this up!

(Photo taken around 1954-1955)

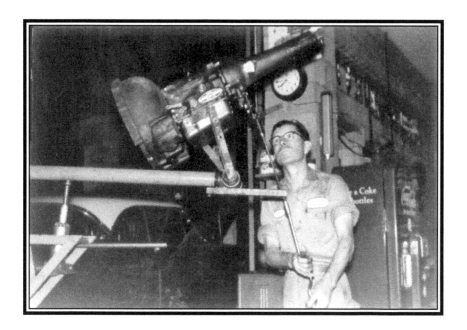

The only photo I have of Daddy at work inside the garage. This one, taken around 1959, shows him busily working on a 52'Ford automatic transmission at about 7:45PM (not that unusual).

Not only did he teach himself how to rebuild automatic transmissions (an extremely complex mechanism) he also designed and built the transmission hoist shown in the picture. This hoist enabled him to remove or install a transmission from the underside of the car with the car six feet in the air on the large hydraulic lift.

This photo, taken in June of 1957, provides a great candid shot of Daddy checking under the hood of what appears to be a 1954 Pontiac Station Wagon. Not captured by the camera are the Gulf gas pumps just to the left or Castleman's Garage just behind the photographer. Also, in the background and just on the other side of the Tennessee Central Railroad tracks are from left to right: the back side of the two story block building which housed the Bank of Mt. Juliet on the ground floor and, on the top floor, the Mt. Juliet Masonic Lodge and Eastern Star (if you look closely you can see the black iron exterior stairway to the second floor which is mentioned in Chapter 1); rear view of the block grocery store to the right of the bank building was, during my Mt. Juliet days, owned by Howard Young, then Sam Jennings and finally Sam Howell; rear view of a white frame building mid-background was part of the grocery's operation and was mostly used to store feed and other non-grocery items also sold by the grocer (very old photos show this building as a one time location for the Mt. Juliet Post Office); the house facing the camera to the right in the background was the Percy Carver home.

A 1946 Mercury receives a replacement radiator from two happy mechanics. From the left, Bobby Begarly (our first cousin who worked for Daddy at Castleman's Garage during the mid-fifties) and my older brother Richard. (photo circa 1954)

Front view of the Oldsmobile engine as it dangled from the chain hoist just moments before it was lowered into the engine compartment of Richard's '48 Ford convertible. The arrows show the custom motor mounts that Daddy welded together from heavy scrap iron.

Rear view of the same engine just before it was bolted to the Ford transmission. The irregularly shaped metal ring that surrounds the hexagon shaped clutch is the special adapter plate (see arrows) that was a key component for the marriage of an Oldsmobile engine to a Ford transmission.

Richard's finished Fordmobile. The top photo beckons you to sit behind the wheel while final adjustments are made under the hood inside Castleman's Garage. Richard was a student at the University of Tennessee in Knoxville when he made the photo at the bottom while his dream car was parked outside the UT football stadium.

Richard and Wynelle Davis (his future bride and my favorite sister-in-law) stand beside of his 1948 "Fordmobile" which is parked in front of the Blockhouse. (photo circa 1956)

CHAPTER 3

From Horseback to Horsepower

FOR THE MOST part, Chapter 2, "Castleman's Garage", was my firsthand account, beginning at about age 4, of my Dad and the family business. The combination of what I've written in this chapter and the photos are an attempt to tell more about my Dad and his career – from the beginning of his life until I began to know him. To write this I relied on what he and others told me along the way. I regret that I asked too few questions and made no notes. Now I can think of a thousand things that I wish I had asked.

In the Beginning

My Dad, Macon Ewing Castleman, was born November 17, 1910 in a rural area of West Wilson County, Tennessee in what is now the southern part of Mt. Juliet. He had two younger siblings, Eunice his brother and Eudelle his sister.

In Daddy's early years, he and everyone he knew traveled by foot, horseback, horse and wagon or horse and buggy.

To the best of my memory, he said he was six or seven before he saw the first automobile. When I asked what the most significant thing was he remembered about that first occasion, he said it was the distinctive smell emitted from the engine. From the moment of that first meeting he was hooked on automobiles.

Until Daddy was around 16, he helped his Father and Mother, Joseph Birdie and Ida Castleman, with farm work. Daddy often said he did not care for farming - and that the long hot days of walking behind a horse drawn plow were enough to convince him that was not the way he wanted to make his living.

In addition to farming, Granddaddy Birdie was a carpenter and owner of a small grocery store on Central Pike. I don't know to what extent Daddy was involved in the grocery store's operation but when he wasn't doing farm work, he and his younger brother Eunice were helping their Dad with carpentry work. (Granddaddy Birdie built several homes that still stand in that area). I would like to believe the early carpentry skills, *et al*, he learned from his Dad were transferable to his ultimate career. Those skills combined with his high intelligence and unbelievable perseverance served as a great platform for his mastery of so many things in which he became intensely interested and naturally good at - just about anything mechanical or electrical.

Midway Garage

There was at least one other man who played a significant role in Daddy's career development. His name was Jonas Newton Carver, aka "Jonie".

On many occasions Daddy told stories about the early part of his career which would begin one of several ways, "Mr. Jonie Carver....", "Jonie Carver..." or "Cousin Jonie Carver..." (he was actually a distant cousin of my Mother whose maiden name was Carver). And the story would always include a mention that "Mr. Jonie" helped give him his start in the auto repair business.

Jonas Newton Carver lived in South Mt. Juliet on the South side of Central Pike just one-half mile east of Mt. Juliet Road. This was within a rock's throw of where my Dad and his family lived.

From the book, *Funeral Records of Jonas Newton Carver* published by the Mt. Juliet –West Wilson County Historical Society, Mr. Carver's granddaughter, Arlene Carver Sturm, wrote this about Jonas:

"A cabinet-maker, he formerly operated a wool carding factory near Mt. Juliet and in 1906 he and a cousin, J. C. Carver,
established the first telephone system in that section, which
they operated for several years. He was, for twenty years, an
undertaker in the area.".

"Across the pike [Central Pike] from his home, he built a little
shop called "Midway Garage". His sons worked on cars in one
part of the building while their "Papa" worked in a separate
area, turning out interesting pieces of furniture and repairing
a variety of things – from dolls to telephones and watches.
One acquaintance recalls that he made the first radio she ever
heard. In the patent office in Washington, D.C. is listed a patent for one of Mr. Carver's inventions, a gadget to be used on
an old-fashioned water tank to prevent the faucet from freezing. In addition, he made many of the caskets for his undertaking business and his wife lined them. He also formed simple
gravestones out of concrete, which included a glass-covered
insert containing a record of the deceased for those who could
not afford a more costly stone."

Having observed my Dad's fascination and passion with everything related to automobiles I have to believe it didn't take long for
he and his brother Eunice to become regular fixtures at Mr. Jonie's
"Midway Garage", especially given its close proximity to their home.
Although I don't know specifically, I believe that between the ages of
about 16 to 20 (1926 to 1930), he and Eunice worked there under

Mr. Jonie's tutelage.

It was not until I was about 13 that I knew "Midway Garage" existed or Daddy's connection with it. Daddy happened to mention that it was the first garage he worked in, so I went by to see it. It was a frame building with a dirt floor and by then (around 1958) it was in pretty bad shape. My trip to see it was productive - I could see the faded white letters that read, "MIDWAY GARAGE". If only I had taken a photo!

As long as I can remember, Daddy was always tinkering with things - taking them apart and putting them back together just to see how they worked - or making his own tools. And, although he never applied for a patent, he very much had an inventor's mind. I have to believe a lot of Mr. Jonie rubbed off on Daddy.

Inside Joseph Birdie Castleman's (my grandfather) first grocery store on the north side of Central Pike. Left to right: Jonas Newton Carver, Joseph Birdie Castleman (holding his pipe in his right hand), Macon Castleman and his brother Eunice Castleman. The subjects are facing west. The doorway to the left (north) led to Jonie Carver's shop. The store's entrance was to the right (south) and faced Central Pike. Midway Garage was located in an adjacent building on the other side of the back wall (east). Circa 1930 (photo courtesy of cousin Carolynn Castleman Payne and description courtesy of family friend Nabe McCulloch).

Tilghman's Stable

Daddy went into the auto repair business on his own on July 4, 1931 - a few months before his 21st birthday. The first Castleman Auto Repair, as it was called at that time, was in the former home of

Tilghman's Stable. This frame building was located near the crossroads in Mt. Juliet at the northeast corner of Mt. Juliet Road and the Old Railroad Bed - now 2145 Mt. Juliet Road. Daddy often mentioned the poor working conditions there – primarily doing auto work on a dirt floor and freezing conditions in the wintertime.

Tilghman's Stable can be seen in the background of the photo above which was made sometime before the NC and St. L Railroad ceased its operation in 1933 (see depot steps and eastbound train at right). A good guess of the photo's date would be sometime between 1924 and 1933 because the newest looking car in the picture, which was heading south on Mt. Juliet Road before it stopped for the train to pass, appears to be of the 1924-1931 vintage. From left to right: Smith and Grigg Store, the old saloon, a gas station and Tilghman's Stable.

The inset below gives a closer look at the building. A building that later stood on this property was previously one of several locations of the Mt. Juliet Post Office.

First location of Castleman Auto Repair beginning July 4, 1931 (formerly Tilghman's Stable).

The $5.00 check below, which is dated September 29, 1931 and payable to Miss Sally Tilgham (endorsed on the back as Sallie Tilgham), shows some early evidence of his expense for building rent.

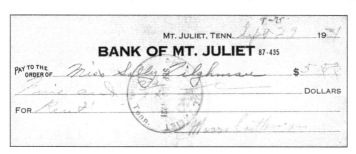

During his days at this location he had a narrow escape with death. He told this story several times and here is how I remember it...

After removing the engine from a car owned by Marion Hardaway, it was decided to push the car back to Marion's house (I presume to get the car out of the way while work was being done on the removed engine). Daddy climbed in Marion's car to steer and Marion pushed him with another car. They moved away from Dad's shop and headed north on Mt. Juliet Road. As they approached the Tennessee Central Railroad crossing a west bound train drew closer and closer. Somehow confusion ensued as to whether they could cross the tracks before the train reached the crossing. The train struck and destroyed the engine-less car Daddy was steering. He was thrown from the car and landed face first in the gravel at the northwest corner of the intersection. He didn't remember much after that. People later told him he was walking around in a very confused state and kept asking what was happening. Since they were not sure of the extent of his injuries beyond the cuts on his face, he was loaded on the train and taken to the hospital in Nashville (probably General) where he remained overnight.

He and my Mom were courting at this time and she worked at the Tennessee School for the Blind (a.k.a. the Blind School) on Hermitage Avenue in Nashville. She got news of the accident and went to see him at the hospital the following morning. By the time she arrived he was lucid and ready to be released. A small scar on his temple was the only permanent evidence of his narrow escape.

Above: These photos, taken on February 22, 1931, provide a great glimpse of Mother and Daddy during their courting days. The car in the background, which Daddy often spoke of with fondness, was his Hubmobile Roadster or the "Hup" as he called it. Thanks to the Antique Car Club of America I determined this was probably a 1924 "Hup" Roadster which had a 4-cylinder engine and disk wheels.

The courtship was successful. R. V. Cawthon married them at Mother's home on June 3, 1933.

The Green Shop

In about 1934, Daddy moved his business across the street to a frame building with a slanted flat roof and a green exterior. The "Green Shop", as he called it, was rented from Toppie McFarland. This building was formally the location for O. E. Philpot's undertaking business (it was used as an embalming facility in the days before there were funeral homes).

The "Green Shop" was located on the West Side of Mt. Juliet Road next door to Toppie McFarland's and across the road from Smith and McCorkle's Store. The only photo I could find was taken from inside the fourth location for Castleman's Garage and it accidentally caught a side view of the "Green Shop" in the background. Richard's black '48 Ford convertible proudly sits to the right of a '53 or '54 Buick.

There are at least three reasons the "Green Shop" enabled Daddy to begin to advance his auto repair capabilities. First of all, repairs were easier because over half of the floor surface was concrete – it was almost a pleasure to jack up a car and crawl under it. Second, Daddy made one major capital improvement. He added a hydraulic automobile lift (grease rack) - but because of the short roof height of the building it was necessary to locate it outside at the front of the building. Third, his advertisements from that era show an effort to connect his business with state-of-the-art equipment and products.

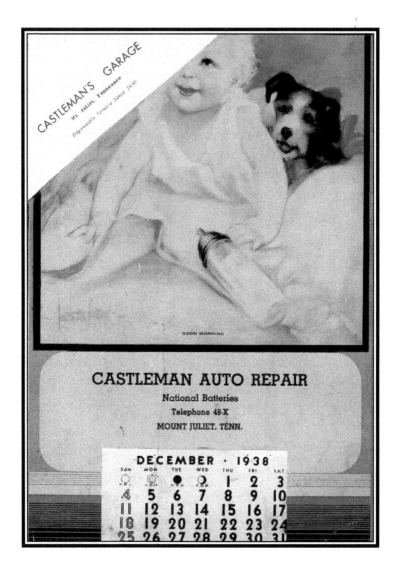

This 1938 calendar is one of my favorite examples of advertising while at the "Green Shop". I don't know why the original top left corner of the calendar was cut away. Daddy placed it in a scrapbook and filled the empty corner with a portion of Castleman's Garage letterhead, which was used in the business from the 50's through the 70's.

Vultee and the "Phillips' Hill Garage

On July 22, 1942 Daddy closed the "Green Shop" and began working in a war time job at Consolidated Vultee Aircraft Company. "Vultee" as it was called was located near Berry Field in Nashville. There his skills and background were used in the final assembly and electrical wiring of two fighter planes, the "Vultee Vengence" and the "P-38 Lightning". His abilities were further recognized by being selected as an instructor and for work in the experimental shop.

An abbreviated version of Castleman Auto Repair continued throughout this period. When he was not working at Vultee he was doing auto repair out of the small stone garage attached to the right end of our home on Phillips' Hill – it too had a dirt floor, which slanted, down the hill.

A close look at the photo below reveals the car parked at the front of the house has no front fenders, hood or radiator. Daddy said he parked it this was so his repair work in progress would be less noticeable.

Other notes about this photo:

1) The Joe Hatfield family owned this land for many years. When Mt. Juliet Road was rerouted from the rear of this property to its current location, Mr. Hatfield built this home to face the new road.

2) On September 16, 1939, Daddy and Mother purchased this new home on "Phillips' Hill" (now 3152 Mt. Juliet Road) from Joe and Mary Hatfield at a cost of $4,000. The purchase price consisted of $2,000 in cash and the deed to the Castleman's Second Avenue home (now 266 Second Avenue), which was valued at $2,000.

3) After the Castlemans and their first two children, Richard and Evalena moved here, three more children arrived – Janice, Bettye and Ronnie. Richard said that when he came downstairs early in the morning and saw Mrs. Walter Phillips (our neighbor across the road) in the living room that it meant another sibling had arrived. Our family has fond memories of this home and we still refer to it as "The house on Phillips' Hill".

Excerpts from Daddy's 1945 desk calendar (shown below) give examples of repair work and names of familiar customers while at the "Phillips' Hill" location. (Note: C = Charged to Account and P = Paid)

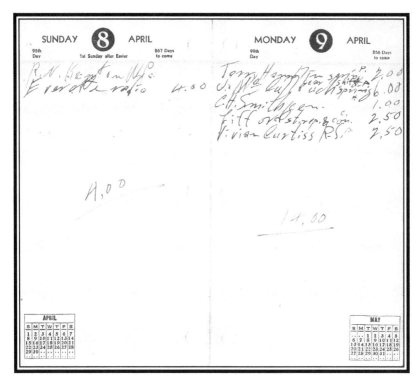

April 8, 1945

- *R. W. Kenton, W. P. (water pump).*
- *Everette, radio $4.00.*
- *(Total revenue before expenses) $4.00*

April 9, 1945

- *Terry Hamblin, spring P. $2.00.*
- *J. McCulloch, gear shift and spring P. $6.00.*
- *C. H. [Hooty] Smith, gen. (generator), $1.00.*
- *Gifford, starter repair and connector, C. $2.50.*
- *Vivian Curtis, R.S. (Road Service), P. $2.50*
- *(Total Revenue before expenses) $14.00*

Castleman's Garage

Daddy left Vultee after the end of World War II and on October 3, 1945, Castleman Auto Repair once again became his full-time endeavor.

He continued operating the business from the little stone garage at his home but began finalizing his plan to relocate to a commercial facility. The plan no longer included a landlord - his goal was to build his own garage.

Even before the end of the war and his departure from Vultee he took the first step to achieve his goal – the purchase of commercial property on which to build his garage. On March 25, 1945, Daddy and Mother bought the "Old Post Office Lot", which was located in the center of Mt. Juliet, from Guy and Lola Murray at a cost of $400. The Mt. Juliet Post Office was located on this property until it burned on February 15, 1942.

In 1946 Daddy and Mother went in debt to have the garage built. Miss Annie Lou McDaniel, manager of the Bank of Mt. Juliet, approved their loan with only their reputations as collateral. Construction began in 1946 and it was completed in 1947.

It was a good structure for its day. The concrete block building had about 4,000 square feet of space and was approximately 25 feet in height. Lots of windows helped provide some natural light. The high ceiling made it possible to locate two hydraulic automobile lifts inside the building so cars could be raised 5 to 6 feet in the air. Two very large doors provided easy entry for cars, tall trucks, buses and farm equipment. If you tried real hard you could squeeze about 6 cars inside

The move to the new building seems to coincide with the evolution of the name of the business – all the advertisements at previous locations used the name "Castleman Auto Repair" and all of the advertisements at this location used the name "Castleman's Garage". And this location was the beginning of the family business I knew and described in Chapter 2. The great experience I had there will always be a valuable part of my underpinning.

The Toolbox

As long as I can remember, Daddy had an old toolbox that sat in front of the small grease rack at Castleman's Garage. I always liked it and mentioned to him that I would like to have it someday.

Sometime after he sold the business and went into semi-retirement, he and Mother drove the 700-mile trip to visit us at our home in Arlington, Texas. They arrived before I got home from work and had already been visiting with my family when I pulled in the driveway. As I walked in the front door and greeted them, Daddy proudly pointed to the old toolbox on the foyer floor. He had cleaned off all the grease, sanded it and painted it a nice glossy black. On the front side he had lettered the following in gold: "Castleman's 1928 - 1978". It was a great way for him to celebrate the 50 or so years he had been in the garage business and make a gift to me at the same time.

He reminded me the toolbox had originally been mounted on the running board of a Model T. He then told me a couple of things I did not know about it. First, he got the toolbox from Mr. Jonie Carver while working with him at "Midway Garage" in the late 1920's. Second, the handle on it was not the original. It was ornate for a toolbox and made of heavy cast metal. Daddy explained that the handle was an extra from Mr. Jonie Carver's casket making and undertaking business.

This toolbox was a silent witness to a man's entire career. It was there during the transition from horseback to horsepower and all the other amazing advances in the auto industry. And it was always in Daddy's view at the front of the hydraulic lift/grease rack, - maybe just to remind him of how it all began and how far things had come.

The toolbox now sits in a prominent corner of my home office. It's one of my prized possessions and one of many treasured icons from my Dad's career.

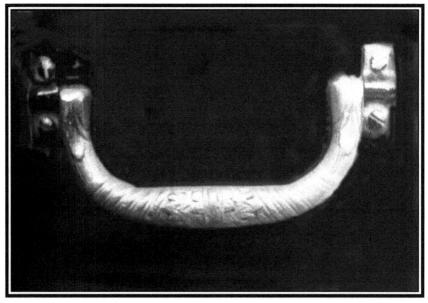

One of Mr. Jonie's surplus caskets handles that found a home on the old tool-box instead of its intended use. Even though the photo could be better a close look shows the intricate casting of the casket handle

CHAPTER 4

The Blockhouse

Background

Between 1855 and 1942 the Mt. Juliet School was located in the heart of the community on what is now known as 130 Second Avenue. There were actually two school buildings located in succession on the same property.

The first school building built in 1855 was closed during the Civil War (1861–1865) so four of the five male teachers could serve in the Confederacy. Three of the four teachers survived and returned to teach when the school reopened.

In 1922 the original frame building was torn away so a more modern brick structure could be built on the very same site. During the construction, classes for the 1922 school year were held in the old mill building located on what is now known as West Division (a.k.a. "The Old Railroad Bed").

The second school building opened in 1923. During most of the school's history it provided classes for grades 1 through 12. In the fall of 1937 it became a grades 1 through 8 school when a new high school was opened just a few a few hundred yards east on Mt. Juliet Road (between the Mt. Juliet Church of Christ and what was then the Mt. Juliet Baptist Church).

Back at that time, Second Avenue was a one-lane dirt road with no official name, but some called it "School Street". It sort of began at the Old Railroad Bed near the old N.C. & St. L. Railroad

Depot (later the Mt. Juliet Telephone Company), and continued for about one-half mile, eventually snaking its way through the school property before ending at Mt. Juliet Road.

The school was a pleasant walk from where the old depot stood. The short distance was filled with three homes on each side of the road. On the right or West Side were the homes of R.V. "Preacher" Cawthon, Miss Carrie Cawthon and Guy Murray, respectively. The three homes on the left belonged, in order, to Miss Annie Grigg, "Dude" Hibbett and my parents (between 1935 and 1939).

The first time people made this walk they may have assumed the road ended at the school's front door. However, as they got closer, they would see that at the front of the school the road made a sharp nine-ty-degree turn to the west. About 100 yards in that same direction was the school's gymnasium, which stood as a separate structure. The football field was located at the rear of the school and ran east to west. Stoner Creek bordered the field on its south side and the Mt. Juliet Church of Christ was just beyond its east goal line.

Tragedy struck around midnight on a very cold Sunday night February 1, 1942 when the school building was completely destroyed by a fire of undetermined origin. Mt. Juliet had no fire department at the time so the flames and smoke from one of the community's largest and most frequently used public structures had to be an un-believable sight. The Guy Murray home, which sat just to the north of the school, was spared that evening by a bucket brigade and a north wind which blew the flames south toward Stoner Creek.

The only thing left from the fire was several hundred feet of the building's solid concrete foundation. It had massive measurements - approximately two feet thick and up to five feet in depth above the ground. Its designer must have also built bomb shelters or owned the company that supplied the cement.

Sometime after the fire," Dude" Hibbett purchased all the school property. He used the football field for growing corn and replaced the gymnasium with a barn. The portion of the property where the school building had stood remained unused and a large amount of the debris from the fire was still evident within the foundation's various boundaries.

In 1948 Mother and Daddy sold our home on Phillips' Hill and began renting a house with no indoor plumbing in the center of Mt. Juliet, which we always referred to as the "Old Yelton Place". The Phillips' Hill Home was sold so they could pay off the business construction loan on Castleman's Garage, which was completed in 1947. What little money they had left was used to purchase two acres of the old school property from Mr. Hibbett. This portion, which included the area where the old school building stood, would eventually become the site of our new home. Mr. Hibbett retained the remainder of the old school property (the cornfield, barn property, etc).

Before I get into the story, there are a couple of small anecdotes I would like to recount. At the time I did not know either event would be a predictor of things to come. Both took place in 1949 when I was four years old. First, I remember an evening when our entire family visited Oakley Smartt's home in Old Hickory so my parents could review the blueprints he'd drawn for what I later learned was our future home. On another occasion, I recall my sister Bettye and me "slipping off" from the Old Yelton Place and somehow ending up at the old school property. During the few minutes it took for our Mother to discover we were missing we played inside the walls of the old foundation and managed to encase our shoes with the gray mud thrown off from a new well that was being dug. I do not recall any punishment or even a mild admonishment. Perhaps Mother was just glad she found us before one of us made our way to the bottom of the well that would eventually supply water to the family.

It was common practice when building a house in those days to build the garage or basement portion to live in first. A few years later the loan for the lot and garage or basement construction could be paid off, or reduced enough, so additional money could be borrowed to build the adjoining house.

Mother and Daddy adopted this approach. In 1949 construction of the home (which would come to be known in our family as "The Blockhouse") began when we built our garage-home.

Unable to take on a traditional mortgage, they borrowed money in bits and pieces and Daddy did much of the work himself. Unfortunately, he could devote only those hours available after putting in an 80-hour workweek in six days at Castleman's Garage. His spare time ended up being mostly on Sunday between church services or late at night.

Some of our construction costs were eliminated because of the ready-made foundation left over from the school. All four walls of what had been the section of foundation for the school's cafeteria were a perfect size and location for our garage-home eleven steps below the level where the house would be built. For the better part of two years the seven of us resided in a mere 622 square feet of living space which consisted of two rooms and a half bath.

The front room had multiple uses. It served as our kitchen, laundry room (wringer washing machine and tubs), eating area and Mother's and Daddy's bedroom. There was just enough room for a chair or two between their bed and the kitchen table. The chairs helped to convert the entire area to another use - our living room when company came.

The large overhead garage door made up most of the left outside wall next to Mother's and Daddy's bed. During the hot days and nights of summer we stayed a little cooler by keeping the overhead door open day and night. Flies, insects and stray dogs and cats were kept away by the custom-made screen Daddy made from light lumber and a long roll of screen wire. I don't know what kept two-legged intruders away, but it didn't much matter because no one locked their doors back then.

The back room was a bedroom for we five children. It included two matching single beds and one set of bunk beds. Being the oldest, Richard got the top bunk, and, during the first few months, Bettye and I shared the lower (she was almost 6 and I was 4). The single beds, which were occupied by Evalena and Janice, were 100% metal fabrication and indestructible. The metal headboards and footboards were painted to look like dark wood - and I think they did - if you were in dim light about 400 hundred feet away! Bettye later got her own bed and because it was a perfect match to the other two, I'm sure it helped to reduce sibling rivalry.

The half-bath the seven of us shared was located in a corner of our bedroom. Every time I visit the lavatory on a commercial airliner it reminds me of the narrow doorway to that tiny bathroom.

Life was not uneventful during our years in the garage. In 1950 Mt. Juliet got its first fire engine (Chapter 6), WSM-TV went on the air (Chapters 10 and 11), and Mother worked as a part-time cook at the school cafeteria.

Since I was only 5 and there was no kindergarten then, my day care consisted of wandering around the school from class to class while Mother worked. I am told it wasn't unusual for me to fall asleep in the corner of a schoolroom while the class went out for recess. Surprisingly, everyone seemed to accept my presence as nothing out of the ordinary.

On Wednesday, January 31, 1951 a six-inch snowfall covered a solid sheet of ice which had formed from a full day of freezing rain and sleet. Temperatures dropped to 1 below zero that night. By Friday of the same week the temperature dropped even further to 13 below. It was so cold the windows in our garage-home iced over inside and out. Many trees were lost in what became known as the "Blizzard of '51" and we, along with most everyone else in Middle Tennessee, had no electricity for about two weeks. The lack of power to our Norge electric range did not stop us from having hot meals. As always Mother overcame that obstacle. She would have said something like, "we'll just have to make do" - which she did by cooking on top of the small butane gas heater that kept us warm. Actually, I think the body heat from seven people in such close quarters also helped to keep us warm.

Another weather-related event occurred during an extremely heavy rainstorm. This time it was at least during warm weather. The back wall of the children's room was a shared foundation wall for what would later be part of our house. Since the house had no walls or roof yet, the four walls of the old open foundation began to collect gallons of water. Unfortunately, the ground sloped in the direction of the back wall of our room. At first we began to notice a little water trickling through the foundation's porous concrete. Mother, Evalena, Janice, Bettye, and I began using rags and buckets to clean up the water. As the water level rose on the opposite side, the volume of water coming through the wall increased and we worked harder and faster. Eventually enough water collected in the open foundation that the floor of our garage home was like a flowing creek at least a foot in depth. We all finally gave up the battle and watched helplessly. Fortunately, we didn't have much of anything that could be ruined by the water. I don't remember being alarmed by all this. I'm guessing that by suppertime it was just another fun event of the day to me.

We had our share of health problems while living in the garage-home as well. Daddy had pneumonia during that time but missed only a few days of work since Castleman's Garage had no group health insurance or sick time benefits. In the fall of 1950, Dr. Lester A. Littell, the town doctor, treated Bettye and Evalena for yellow jaundice. Bettye's case was severe enough that she missed 6 weeks or so of school. I think we all envied that her bed was moved to the front room so Mother could take care of her during the night - or maybe it was to minimize the risk of contagion.

Construction of our new blockhouse seemed to move at glacier speed.

Daddy chose concrete blocks for the exterior walls. While this was (and still is) a very uncommon material for a home's exterior, blocks were chosen because they were cheaper than bricks both in terms of labor and materials. I know of only one other home built in Mt. Juliet where concrete blocks were used for the exterior walls. Daddy started the block work himself but gave up quickly. He finally subcontracted the work to Algee Clemmons, a local mason.

The roof, interior walls and plastering was also subcontracted. However, Daddy hung all the doors, did all the electrical and plumbing work and installed the kitchen cabinets. He and Mother laid, sanded and stained the hardwood floors. The particular grade of hardwood flooring they purchased was so hard neither of them could drive a nail in the tongue of the wood without bending it. I can still see Mother very ably using a 3/8-inch electric drill to make small pilot holes so finishing nails wouldn't bend as she drove them in. They also put down the vinyl tile in the kitchen and bath.

Our house only used a small portion of the school's original foundation and hundreds of feet were left unused and exposed at the front as well as the East Side. It was fascinating to watch how this issue was solved. Spider Stewart, who worked for Jones Brothers' Construction Company, used a bulldozer which towed a very large earth moving pan to move huge quantities of dirt from an area near Stoner Creek. The dirt was then spread over the unused foundation to create a level yard around the front of our house.

In 1951, the year I started to school, the walls and roof on the blockhouse were finally finished. The seven of us were more than eager to move upstairs from our two-room garage-home to a real house with six rooms and a full bathroom. This eagerness was manifested on at least two occasions.

A large heavy crate was delivered to the back of the house that we soon discovered contained a white porcelain bathtub. This was more than exciting to some family members because our garage-home had only a half-bath. I, on the other hand, had no interest in baths whether they were full or half.

Eventually the tub was uncrated and somehow moved up the eleven wood steps at the back of the house and into the area that would become the bathroom. Before the plumbing to the tub could be completed, at least one of my sisters (I believe it was Evalena) used the hosepipe to fill the tub with cold water for a bath. After bathing from only a wash basin for over two years, even a cold tub bath had to have been sheer luxury. I'm pretty sure the weather was fairly warm at the time so I don't think anyone turned blue.

Later that year we also demonstrated our eagerness to move upstairs by celebrating our first Christmas (1951) in the unfinished room that would later become our kitchen.

By 1952, construction of the blockhouse had progressed to the "just barely habitable" point so we could move up from our garage-home down below. There was still much to be done at the point of move-in, but it didn't matter to any of us. By saying "barely habitable" I mean the interior doors were yet to be hung, etc., etc.

For a number of years, the concrete block exterior of the house remained unpainted. I'm sure this was for several reasons. First, it was probably thought concrete blocks need not be preserved and paint was for esthetic purposes only. Secondly, the paint could be bought after some of the debt had been paid. And finally, Daddy would be the one doing the painting in his minimal spare time, which was already absorbed by the completion of other interior finish-out work.

The lack of any paint on the concrete blocks proved to be a costly mistake. We were plagued for years by plastered interior walls that would blister and peel underneath each windowsill inside the house. Since concrete blocks are porous, a sweating condition resulted on the inside of the house during cold weather. The plaster problem was extremely upsetting and frustrating for Daddy, and he spent many Sundays patching and re-patching the unsightly appearance inside our home. He was very vocal about how much this problem bothered him. Daddy was a highly intelligent and ingenious person who could fix just about anything. This was something he couldn't seem to beat, and I wish it hadn't troubled him so much.

It wasn't until the mid-fifties that the plaster problem was solved. First Mother and Daddy borrowed the money to replace our butane gas heaters with a central butane furnace that blew warm air to a register underneath each window...this was nice! Next, Daddy found the time and a product (ThoroughSeal) that would both seal and paint the exterior of the concrete blocks. Finally, he began to custom make storm windows to cover each of our extremely large windows. The construction of custom-made storm windows was tedious and very time consuming. After making two of them he finally paid Robert Jones, a local craftsman, to make the remainder, along with wood windowsills for the interior.

The solution to the plaster problem was a huge load off Daddy and I think that part of his life was finally better. I know he and Mother were pleased with the results.

During the years following our move upstairs to the Blockhouse, our garage-home below was used for several purposes. First, the dividing wall between the front and back room was removed so it could be used as a meeting and dining area for the Mt. Juliet Men's Club. Every Tuesday evening Mother prepared supper for 20 or so attendees. My sisters helped with the serving, clean up, etc. While all this was going on Truman Hibbett, Charles Lee McCorkle, Richard and I would eat the same meal as the Men's Club but did so in our house upstairs while watching shows like "Milton Berle" on TV.

The Men's Club was always working on something that would improve the community, e.g. the volunteer fire department, lighting for the football field, safe drinking water, etc. One of these endeavors in the fall of 1952 ended up causing them to move their Tuesday night meetings to the school cafeteria.

When Dr. Littell moved away from Mt. Juliet around 1952, the Men's Club convinced three Nashville medical doctors to provide limited afternoon office hours in Mt. Juliet. The next challenge was where the doctors would be located. Somehow what had originally been our garage-home, and now the meeting place for the Men's Club, was chosen. The following is a copy of the announcement card Mother kept:

```
THE MT. JULIET MEN'S CLUB
wishes to announce they have arranged with three Nashville doctors to
hold office hours in Mt. Juliet daily, Monday through Friday, from 4 to 6 pm.
The office will be located in the rear of the

MACON CASTLEMAN HOME IN MT. JULIET
Telephone 881-W.

The doctors and the times they will be here are:
DR. WALTER L. DIVELEY - SURGERY, Tues. and Thurs.

DR. JAMES W. ELLIS - OBSTETRICS and
GYNECOLOGY - Friday

DR. CLARENCE C. WOODCOCK - MEDICINE
Monday and Wednesday

The office hours will begin Monday, October 6, 1952
```

My first inkling that the clinic was about to happen was when a truck backed up to the back door of our house and unloaded a physician's examination table, a sterilizer and other medical equipment onto our garage floor. What had been the bedroom for the five of us during the garage-home days became one-third doctors office and two-thirds examination room. What had been the front room was used as a waiting room for patients.

The small doctor's office had four walls and a door, but the exam room was separated from the waiting area by only a heavy curtain. This feature of the clinic made me nervous and I felt the exam room should have had a real wall. Fortunately, I never had to be examined.

Although Mother was no longer preparing meals for the Men's Club, she now had a new job (among her many others) of assisting the doctors with patients. The Doctors had no nurse so Mom admitted patients, sterilized needles, was present for the examination of female patients, etc.

The Mt. Juliet Clinic didn't last very long and many people in Mt. Juliet never knew it existed. Years later Mother said one thing the doctors complained about was the drive between Nashville and Mt. Juliet for only two hours of office time. At that time, Highway 70 was the main road to and from Nashville, which meant lots of traffic passing on a two-lane road, and there was of course the infamous "S" curve (in Davidson County between Donelson and Nashville).

After the clinic was gone and the doctor's office and the curtain were removed, we finally began to use the garage for its intended purpose, at least for a little while.

By the time I was about 12 Richard had grown up and left home and I had our room all to myself. Evalena, Janice and Bettye had grown very tired of sharing one of the three bedrooms and Evalena was ready for a room of her own. This was a great opportunity to have my own room downstairs in part of our old garage-home. Daddy put up a new wall and door and recreated what had been the bedroom for we five Castleman kids. Now I had the old back room all to myself and Mother parked her car in what had been the front room.

I sort of had my own garage apartment with a private entrance. I lived just like Oscar Madison on the TV series "The Odd Couple", only I was a lot messier. Mother finally gave up on my problem of never picking anything up off the floor. I was in heaven!

My description of life during the garage-home years is not meant to imply that this was a hardship situation. It would be hard to live that way now but I thought nothing of it at the time and I enjoyed every minute of it. Would I go back and change any of that experience? Absolutely not!

It took Mother and Daddy years of incredibly hard work to finish the Blockhouse. I really appreciate that and the 16 years we were there. I learned so much!

Mother and Daddy sold the Blockhouse in March of 1965 and bought a new home.

Mt. Juliet School 1855-1922. This school was torn away in 1922 so the new school (see photo below) could be built on the same location. Circa 1907.

Mt. Juliet School around 1923. It was completely destroyed by fire on Sunday, February 1, 1942. In 1949 it became the site of the Blockhouse.

Mt. Juliet from the air after the Second Avenue School was destroyed by fire. 1. Baptist Church; 2. High School; 3. Vocational Agriculture Shop; 4. Church of Christ; 5. Football Field; 6. Old School Site (Second Avenue School) and location of our future home; 7. Old School Well; 8. First Gymnasium; 9. Tennis Court; 10. Guy Murray Home. (photo taken some time between February 1, 1942 and October 23, 1946.

The inset shows the exposed foundation and smokestack, which were the only remains of the Second Avenue School (#6). The school cafeteria, which was located in the small rectangular section of foundation just to the left of the smokestack, would later become the garage-home portion of the Blockhouse. (photo taken some time between 1942 and 1946)

The old school foundation, which was made of solid concrete, met the new concrete blocks at the bottom of our bedroom window in the garage-home. The beginning of a corner of the Blockhouse is shown immediately behind Evalena and me. (clockwise: Evalena, Janice, Bettye and me).

I couldn't resist including this photo of the five of us taken on the same day as the previous photo. Each one of us was having a problem with the sun! Bettye is really our sister and not an adopted orphan from Holland. Actually, she was in a school play that day. (clockwise: Evalena, Janice, Richard, Bettye and me).

Suppertime in our garage-home in January 1950. Left to right – Richard, Janice, Mother, me, Bettye and Evalena.

Christmas morning (Tuesday, December 25, 1951) in the unfinished kitchen of the Blockhouse while we were still living downstairs in the garage. Kitchen cabinets, our stove and refrigerator would later line the two walls shown. Evalena and I were enjoying my toys. That was a great Christmas!

The Blizzard which began January 31, 1951.

Top – looking north on Second Avenue toward the Mt. Juliet Telephone Office which was formerly the N.C. & St. L Railroad Depot.

Bottom – two of our neighbors trying to keep warm. N.C. Hibbett, Jr. and his Mom, Mrs. Cliffodene.

More pictures from the Blizzard of '51. Top - Evalena (L) and Janice (R) beside the Blockhouse which had its roof and walls, but we were still living in the garage. The Guy Murray home is in the background. Bottom - Only the barely visible car tracks remind you there is a driveway where Bettye and I are playing. Hibbett's barn is in the upper left of the photo.

Xmas 1963

Look closely and you'll see Santa greeting you at the front door of the "Blockhouse" on Second Avenue On the back of this photograph Mother simply wrote the note above. In the Wednesday, December 25, 1963 issue of the Nashville Tennessean columnist Julie Hollabaugh wrote, "It's Colorful, White and Cold…many have their wish for a White Christmas".

The photo above shows a snow scene at the same location years earlier when it was the Mt. Juliet School on Second Avenue. (Photo courtesy of Ruby Murray Gumz)

CHAPTER 5

Scrapbook of Nine Fiery Years

I'VE ALWAYS BEEN interested in knowing more details about some of the major fires that took place in Mt. Juliet prior to the establishment of its first fire department in 1950. Most of this interest stems from two events that had a significant impact on my life. In 1946, "Castleman's Garage" was built on the site of the Mt. Juliet Post Office, which burned in 1942. And, in 1949 "The Blockhouse" was built on the site of the Mt. Juliet Elementary School, which also burned in 1942.

This chapter is a look back at not only those two fires but three others as well, all five of which occurred between 1938 and 1946. The fires I'm referring to destroyed (in chronological order):

-   The Mt. Juliet Baptist Church (now 2030 N. Mt. Juliet Road),
-   The Mt. Juliet Elementary School on Second Avenue (now 130 Second Ave),
-   The Mt. Juliet Post Office Building (now 108 West Division Street),
-   The Mt. Juliet High School (now a parking lot between 1940 and 2030 N. Mt. Juliet Road)
-   And, for the second time, The Mt. Juliet Baptist Church (2030 N. Mt. Juliet Road).

The cumulative effect of these losses and others was the driving force that brought fire protection to the community.

I have heard people talk about these fires with great frequency but have no firsthand memory – three of them occurred a few years before I was born and two happened when I was too young to remember. On many occasions I heard Richard and Evalena recount what it was like in 1946 when their school burned and then subsequently having classes in the Sunday School rooms at the Mt. Juliet Church of Christ.

It is a sad thought when you think about what it must have been like for the people of Mt. Juliet to lose one of their community buildings. These structures were important gathering places, filled with wonderful memories, and the heart and soul of the community. Suffice it to say the tragic losses that are about to be described would have ripped the heart out of most communities. However, the strength and perseverance of the citizens of Mt. Juliet overcame each of these setbacks. As a result I think each loss and disruption made community loyalty even stronger.

Rather than attempt to tell these stories in my own words, the following pages include copies of actual newspaper clippings from *The Lebanon Democrat* and *The Donelson Diary*, photos and a few other notes I've compiled to create sort of a scrapbook of this historic period.

This chapter is dedicated to all the people who lived through and overcame these tragic events that had such a negative impact on the community. I may be better off that I don't remember the fires, but I'm glad to have known the people who did. The people of Mt. Juliet showed great courage and fortitude during this period.

Mt. Juliet Baptist Church, 9:45 AM - Sunday, March 6, 1938

One of the first fires in this time period occurred in 1938. The following is an excerpt from the *Chronological History of the First Baptist Church –Mt. Juliet* by N.C. Hibbett, Jr.

"On Sunday morning, March 6, 1938, about 9:45, the church building burned. Many of us will never forget the sound the large church bell made as it fell. The people were in great shock until friends from Cloyds Cumberland Presbyterian Church put forth the hand of friendship by inviting us to worship with them.

That afternoon the church met for discussing plans for the future. The public school was offered as a meeting place until other plans could be made, and the church voted to accept the offer. Mr. R. R. Rummage gave the first donation for a new building".

> *"That same night a second conference was held. The minutes read as follows: Mr. Walter Phillips was appointed as a committee of one to buy coal to be used when meeting in the school building. H. W. Young, church clerk, was appointed to represent the church in the settlement with the insurance company. At the request of the pastor, Humphrey McCorkle made [a] motion that the pastor appoint a building committee of seven men to draw plans, to survey and to build a new church. [The] Motion carried. The following committee was appointed: V. G. Hawkins, Chairman, J. A. Gifford, H. W. Young, Walter Phillips, Edgar Curd, Rollie Peek and Travis Garret".*

"On March 20, 1938, the church met to discuss plans for a new church. T.L. Clemons brought to the church a set of plans for consideration. The plans were accepted, and the church instructed the committee to place the church as near the center of the lot as possible."

Mt. Juliet Baptist Church destroyed by fire
9:45 AM, Sunday, March 6, 1938.
(Photo circa 1936)

Mt. Juliet Elementary School Destroyed, 11:00 PM – Sunday, February 1, 1942

Just a little less than four years had passed when on Sunday, February 1, 1942 the Mt. Juliet Elementary School (where the "Blockhouse" described in Chapter 4 was later built and what is now known as 130 Second Avenue) was destroyed by fire around 11:00 PM. Following the fire, the grammar school students were transferred to quarters in the Mt. Juliet High School Building and the Mt. Juliet Baptist Church.

An early photo of the Mt. Juliet School (Second Avenue) 1922 – 1942

Mt. Juliet Elementary School Destroyed, 11:00 PM – Sunday, February 1, 1942 (continued) Lebanon Democrat - Thursday, February 5, 1942

Mt. Juliet School Is Destroyed by Fire

BUILDING AND CONTENTS ARE TOTAL LOSS: ORIGIN OF FIRE UNDETERMINED.

A disastrous fire of undetermined origin completely destroyed the brick veneer grammar school building at Mt. Juliet, Sunday night, causing losses estimated as high as $40,000. The building and its contents, includin the school auditorium and cafeteria equipment, was a total loss.

The fire was reported at midnight by Mrs. Sam Bond, Mt. Juliet telephone operator. Prof. Paul Lindsey and Howard Young, a member of the school board reported that when they arrived on the scene the blaze was beyond control Nothing was saved from the building.

The building was insured for $10,000, Young reported Monday morning. As far as could be learned early this week no insurance at all was carried on the contents of the building, including desks, electric applionece and other school room equipment. The building was owned by the Mt. Juliet special school district, and was completed in 1923 at a cost of $22,000.

It was reported that no fire had been built in the building since school was dismissed Friday, and there was no clue as to how the fire may have started. The left wing of the building collapsed first, it was said, indicating that the fire started in that part of the building.

Arrangements were completed Monday to have the grammar school students transferred to quarters in the high school building and the Baptist church, members of the school board stated. Approximately 450 pupils were enrolled in the school.

Members of the special school district board are Howard Young, Herman Agee, Folyd Smartt, J. C. Spence and T. E. Weston.

Mt. Juliet Elementary School Destroyed, 11:00 PM – Sunday, February 1, 1942 (continued)

The following photos and excerpt from a tribute on page 4 of the 1941-1942 yearbook, the *Golden Leaf*, appropriately describes some of the feelings of sadness as a result of the loss of this school:

"A few months ago, disaster in the form of fire destroyed the grammar school building... a great loss as to property value as well as a center of community activity. .... there was one thing which it could not destroy, the institution of learning housed there; it only caused it to move elsewhere. .... we wish to pause and express our gratitude to this institution for the knowledge received there and for the character-building which is the molder of our lives".

Before....

Now Ruins....

Mt. Juliet Post Office Destroyed, 11:00 PM - Sunday, February 15, 1942

Exactly two weeks later, on Sunday, February 15, 1942, the Mt. Juliet Post Office Building (where Castleman's Garage was later located) was destroyed by fire. This fire like the one a fortnight earlier at the Mt. Juliet Baptist Church also occurred around 11:00 PM. *Left article Lebanon Democrat, Thursday, February 19, 1942. Related article on right, Lebanon Democrat February 26, 1942.*

Postoffice Building At Mt. Juliet Is Destroyed by Fire

Mt. Juliet's second disastrous fire in two weeks completely destroyed the two-story postoffice building Sunday night. The building and its contents were a total loss, with losses estimated at from $5,000 to $7,000. J. A. Gifford, owner of the building, said that the loss was partially covered by insurance amounting to approximately half the value of the property.

The building burned at 11 o'clock Sunday night, exactly two weeks after the $40,000 fire which destroyed the Mt. Juliet grammar school. The fact that both fires occurred at about the same hour on Sunday night, of undetermined causes. caused some speculation in the community as to whether or not the fires were started by a "fire bug" arsonist. However, in so far as was known, no person is suspected of having started the fires.

In addition to the postoffice, the building was, occupied by the offices of Squire A. A. Alexander, a barber shop operated by Joe Hunt, and a lodge hall used by the Eastern Star and the Masonic chapter.

It was reported that the fire started in the barber shop. On account of the loss of federal property in the postoffice, it was considered likely that the FBI might investigate the case.

HUNT BARBER SHOP OPEN FOR BUSINESS

Mr. Joe Hunt, barber, is now in business in the new building recently erected by A. L. Partee. Mr. Hunt's shop has been completely destroyed by fire twice within the past year.

Mt. Juliet Post Office Destroyed, 11:00 PM - Sunday, February 15, 1942 (continued)

As can be seen, the Old Post Office Building (3) had two floors. The Post Office was on the ground floor and faced the Tennessee Central Railroad Tracks. Joe Hunt's Barbershop faced Mt. Juliet Road, as did the steps that led upstairs to the Masonic Lodge and Eastern Star. A. A. "Dick" Alexander was a Notary Public and his office faced south and the building that would subsequently become the next post office and Jordan's Store Building.

Castleman's Garage was built on the Old Post Office property in 1946 (see Chapter 2). Other landmarks in the photo include: (1) Log yard; (2) Railroad Foreman's Section House; 3. Old Post Office Building (4) Tennessee Central Railroad Depot; (5) Coal House; (6) Back of Smith and Grigg Store; (7) N.C. and St. L. Railroad Depot.

Mt. Juliet High School Destroyed, 3:00 AM - Wednesday, October 23, 1946

At around 3:00 AM on Wednesday, October 23, 1946 the Mt. Juliet High School was destroyed by fire. This school was located on Mt. Juliet Road between the Mt. Juliet Church of Christ and the Mt. Juliet Baptist Church. This location is now a parking lot between 1940 and 2030 N. Mt. Juliet Road.

Front page, Lebanon Democrat October 24, 1946
(article continued on next page)

Because the Mt. Juliet Grammar School had burned four years and eight months earlier, both the high school and grammar school students were being cared for in the high school building, which was crowded beyond its capacity.

Construction of the new elementary school had begun several weeks prior to the high school fire but it was several months from completion.

Mt. Juliet High School Destroyed, 3:00 AM - Wednesday, October 23, 1946 (continued)

Front page, Lebanon Democrat October 24, 1946

BRICK STRUCTURE RAZED BY FLAMES EARLY YESTERDAY

The second disaster in four years hit the Mt. Juliet schools when the high school building and contents were completely destroyed by fire of unknown origin about 3 o'clock Wednesday morning. The elementary school building was totally destroyed by in February, 1942.

The fire was discovered about 3 o'clock by Mrs. E. L. Still, who lives near the school. The fire seemed to be in the library, it is stated. School officials believe that faulty wiring must have been the cause.

The building, a one-story brick veneer, was built in 1936 at a cost of $35,000. It contained ten rooms and a large, well-equipped gymnasium. The building was insured for the full cost of $35,000, and the contents for $3,000, James E. Belcher, county superintendent of education, announced. However, it is estimated that cost of replacement will run in excess of $70,000 at prices prevailing today, Belcher said. The school vault, containing records and other valuables, was saved.

"We will do the best we can, but at the present time I see no facilities available to take care of the 460 students who were attending the school," Belcher said.

Construction of the new elementary school began several weeks ago, and is about half completed. It will take several months yet to get the building ready for occupancy, it is stated.

Both high school and elementary students were being cared for in the high school, which was crowded far beyond its capacity.

The only way to take care of the students is to scatter them among the other schools of the county, and most of the other schools are crowded, officials state.

No statement was made as to whether or not a special session of the county court might be asked for to consider replacement of the building.

The call was answered by Engine No. 10 from Nashville, which is said to have made the run in 12 minutes. Owing to a breakdown in one of Lebanon's engines, the call could not be answered from here.

Mt. Juliet High School Destroyed, 3:00 AM - Wednesday, October 23, 1946 (continued)

The first sentence in the last paragraph of the news clipping on the previous page amazes me: "The call was answered by Engine No. 10 from Nashville, which is said to have made the run in 12 minutes".

With Highway 70 as the only route between Nashville and Mt. Juliet at that time, a 12-minute run would have been a suicide ride. The futile attempt by the Nashville Fire Department further underscores how desperately Mt. Juliet needed its own fire department.

Mt. Juliet High School – 1938 – 1946

An article in the October 31, 1946 edition of the Lebanon Democrat underscores how the local citizenry began to rebuild.

Mt. Juliet Residents Raise Funds For School Equipment

Residents of Mt. Juliet chipped in a total of $3,100 Tuesday night to purchase equipment for the burned high school, and earmarked $1,000 of the sum as a reward for the conviction of the firebug who might have been responsible for the fires there.

With an attendance of approximately 300, an organization was effected to work to raise funds not only to get equipment, but also to apply on the new buildings which must be erected to replace the one destroyed by fire last week, it was announced. J. C. Spence was named chairman, J. B. Falkner secretary, and R. V. Cawthon treasurer.

The group plans a box supper Friday night, which will be held at the Green Hill club house. Proceeds will be used for the school.

T. L. Clemmons, architect, attended the meeting Tuesday night, and presented plans for the new school building.

At the present time, students are being housed in the Cloyd's Presbyterian church, Baptist church, the Church of Christ, and in a work shop of the former high school.

"If windows are released to the contractors, we will be able to get in the elementary school within sixty days," James E. Belcher, county superintendent, stated yesterday.

Mt. Juliet Baptist Church Destroyed, 6:00 PM, Thursday, November 14, 1946

The healing and recovery process had just begun when at 6:00 PM on Thursday, November 14, 1946, the Mt. Juliet Baptist Church was destroyed by fire. Ironically the Baptist Church was one of the temporary locations (see article on previous page) that housed some of the students who lost their school building three weeks earlier.

Mt. Juliet Baptist Church, 1938 - 1946

As can be seen on the following pages of newsprint, it was not long before multiple investigations uncovered a suspect and the full confession from an 18-year-old male resident of Mt. Juliet.

NOVEMBER 21, 1946

18-year Old Is Mt. Juliet Fire Starter

CONFESSES TO 2 RECENT FIRES BUT GIVES NO REASON

An 18-year-old youth, believed to be mentally deficient, was the self-confessed "Mt. Juliet fire-bug," according to highway patrol officials who conducted an investigation and brought about the boy's arrest Monday evening of this week.

The youth is Woodrow Wilson Still, son of W. G. Still, a Nashville auto mechanic. The family moved to Mt. Juliet in March of this year and are not well known in the community. His mother was to arrive today from Baltimore, Maryland, where she has been visiting recently.

Mt. Juliet's series of fires have long been cause for talk in Wilson and Davidson counties, they starting back in March, 1938, when the Baptist Church burned. Later, in February, 1942, the Grammar School burned and was followed by a three-story building in March that housed the Post Office, a garage and grocery store and also the local lodge rooms. Suspects were questioned at that time but no confessions were obtained and the community gradually forgot the incidents.

High School Burns

On October 23 of this year, late at night, the community was startled from sleep by the burning of the High School. Investigations were conducted but led nowhere. Then, last Thursday evening at 6 o'clock, November 14, the community was called out again— the Baptist church was in flames.

Investigations were started immediately. Buell Agee, local constable, conducted his privately, another was headed by Wilson county Sheriff Ewing Atkinson, still another was led by State Fire Commissioner R. K. Webb, and finally one was headed by Sgt. Bill Williams and Patrolman Elmer Craig of the Tennessee State Highway Patrol. It was the latter two men's investigation who brought about the arrest of young Still and his ultimate admittance to the two recent fires.

As quickly as possible after last Thursday's fire Deputy Jim Marable, of the State Penitentiary, assisted by Dave White, brought the state's bloodhounds to the scene and they shortly picked a trail that led first to a barn at the rear of the property of Herbert Talbot, a former Mt. Juliet school bus driver. When the dogs refused to go further, they were led on another trail and by a circuitous route, almost a mile and a half in length, they went to the front door of Ernest Weston, former school board member of the Mt. Juliet system. Neither man was questioned at the time but investigations continued with virtually everyone in Mt. Juliet under suspicion, not openly accusing anyone, but eyeing and talking about almost everyone else.

Tells of Actions

Monday evening of this week Sgt. Williams went to the Green Hill Church of Christ, where was housed the 7th grade of Mt. Juliet, and called out young Still, one of the class. After gentle talking and discussing, the youth admitted the two fires and told how he had crept down a creaky stairs after his parents had gone to bed, gone to the school house and torn up books and old papers and ignited the fire that destroyed the

(Continued on page 6)

PAGE 6

Mt. Juliet Fire--
(Continued from page 1)

building. He returned to his house, crept back up the stairs and watched out his window at the flames spreading, finally arousing his father as the general alarm was sounded. Young Still repeated his story to a DIARY reporter from his cell in the Wilson county jail again on Tuesday of this week and professed he did not know why he committed the crime.

Last Thursday, Still continued his story, he went to the Baptist Church via the main road, entered the building evidently only shortly after Howard Young, Mt. Juliet merchant, had been in the building, and in a small room at the rear used more for storage than anything else, he lit the curtain on the window. It is thought flames from it ignited oil and paint in the room causing the fire to spread so rapidly.

Following both fires young Still had worked with others in preparing new school rooms, outdoor latrines and water lines so that school might be continued. He professed a liking for his teacher, his principal, and his fellow students, and could only say he was sorry for what he had done and sorry he caused so much loss.

In the meantime young Still sits in the Wilson county jail awaiting trial, which is doubtful as to when it will be called. In all probability, by admission of his father, and by talking with his teachers, the boy is not considered 'too bright.' A neat, well mannered and nice looking lad, he has been handicapped by a childhood illness that forced him many grades behind in his school studies. In all probability, according to Sheriff Atkinson, the boy will be committed to an institution for the mentally deficient.

Still Keep Watch

Now, Mt. Juliet hopes its fire troubles are over, however, there are still skeptics in the community who feel young Still isn't guilty, and Mt. Juliet as a whole is keeping its lights on full at night. Insurance has been increased on virtually all buildings, including the Green Hill Church of Christ where young Still was in school.

Too, the Mt. Juliet School Equipment Association was recently formed with J. C. Spence as its head, and a goal of $15,000 was set by the community to raise to equip a new High School. Almost half has been pledged, and the group hopes to complete the goal within the next month. With that much for equipment for a new school, members of the group feel they will then be able to go to the Wilson County Court and receive their approval of funds to build a new building at Mt. Juliet so school may be properly conducted in the old fashion. Just across the road from the proposed and hoped-for site, a new Grammar School nears completion with occupancy some two or three months away.

A reward of $1,600 offered by the Association will be received by the two state highway patrolmen for their finding the arsonist but, as state employees cannot receive rewards of this nature, they will accept it only in token and then return the money, half going toward the new school equipment and half to the Baptist Church Building Fund.

The Lebanon Democrat's front page included four articles related to the fires. Because the newsprint is small, the "Confession Ends", article in the rigtht column is enlarged on the next thrcc pages.

Mt. Juliet Rebuilding Plans Made; Boy Confesses Fires

Board Studies Plans For New Mt. Juliet School Building

Tentative plans for the construction of a high school building at Mt. Juliet to replace the one destroyed by fire on October 23 were made at the meeting of the county board of education held Monday, James E. Belcher, county superintendent of education, announced.

It is planned to build the high school on to the present elementary school now under construction, with the auditorium and class rooms directly to the rear, and the gymnasium at the rear, and to the side, it is stated. The same type of material used in the elementary school would be used.

It was pointed out by Thomas L.

Apologies Accepted

Members of the county court who attended the meeting of the county board of education Monday voted unanimously to accept the apologies of the Lebanon High school faculty for the article which appeared in the student publication recently.

Carl J. Chaney, principal, spoke briefly, explaining the circumstances as to how the article appeared without their knowledge, and extended the apologies of the faculty.

Clemmons, architect who drew the plans, that this would not only save original cost of construction, but would make a considerable savings during the years in maintenance costs.

Both the elementary building and proposed high school building are so arranged that additions could be made to them when increased enrollment makes it necessary, the architect stated. These buildings will be absolutely fireproof.

Estimated cost of the proposed building will be ready by the time the board of education meets next month, Belcher stated.

$15,000 Sought By Mt. Juliet Group For School Equipment

A drive to raise $15,000 in the Mt. Juliet section of the county has been launched by the Mt. Juliet School Equipment committee, which was organized immediately after the high school building was destroyed by fire, J. C. Spence, chairman, announced yesterday.

At the organization meeting held after the high school burning, the citizens pledged $3,100, $1,000 of which was earmarked as a reward for the arrest and conviction of the person responsible for the fire. This was later raised to $1,500.

"We realize that the county has been hard hit in these disasters, and we feel that it is up to the citizens of the Mt. Juliet community to do all they can themselves before going to the county court and asking for replacement of the school facilities," Spence stated.

Lists of contributors to this fund will be published in The Democrat.

Children's Chairs Sought by JCC

Small chairs for use by the little children of the first three grades of the Mt. Juliet school will be collected by the Lebanon Jaycees in a house-to-house canvass of Lebanon Sunday morning, December 1, before church hours.

After the Mt. Juliet school burned, the citizens of that area gave the school all the small chairs available there, and the burning of the Baptist church, which housed the younger classes, destroyed the results of this drive—there's not a small chair left in that entire section of the county.

"Search your attics and basements thoroughly for small straight chairs for the children," President J. B. Leftwich urged. "Put them on the front porch or at the curb the morning of December 1 and we will collect them."

Grateful for the aid offered by the Lebanon club, Mrs. A. A. Alexander, Mt. Juliet principal, described the desperate need of the school:

"You should see these little children sitting on grown-ups' chairs; their feet can't touch the floor and they get so tired before the day is over," she said.

Confession Ends Four-Day Search For Arson Culprit

The destruction of both the Mt. Juliet elementary school and the Mt. Juliet Baptist church by fire was admitted Monday night by William Wilson Still, 18-years-old student in the Mt. Juliet grammar school, in a confession made to State Safety Commissioner Lynn Bomar, Sgt. Bill Williams, and Patrolman Elmer V. Craig of the state highway patrol in the presence of the boy's father, Emmitt L. Still, Nashville auto mechanic.

The boy was turned over to Sheriff Ewing Atkinson at the county jail Monday night by the state officers and H. W. Young, Mt. Juliet merchant who assisted in the investigation, and warrant charging young Still with arson on two counts was issued by Magistrate W. H. Conatser.

The Stills moved to Mt. Juliet only a few months ago, and live just across the road from the burned school building.

Discovery that the Stills had suffered from two fires in the past—their home in Nashville and their chicken house in Mt. Juliet had both been burned—caused the officer to question the boy, who had been at home alone on both occasions.

While Williams admitted setting fire to the school and the church, he insisted he had nothing to do with the fires at his home.

In the confession, he said that on the night the school burned (October 23) he arose about two or three o'clock, went to the kitchen of his home across the road to the school.

"I pushed up a window and climb-

(Continued on Page 5)

Confession Ends Four-Day Search For Arson Culprit

The destruction of both the Mt. Juliet elementary school and the Mt. Juliet Baptist church by fire was admitted Monday night by William Wilson Still, 18-years-old student in the Mt. Juliet grammer school, in a confession made to State Safety Commissioner Lynn Bomar, Sgt. Bill Williams, and Patrolman Elmer V. Craig of the state highway patrol in the presence of the boy's father, Emmitt L. Still, Nashville auto mechanic.

The boy was turned over to Sheriff Ewing Atkinson at the county jail Monday night by the state officers and H. W. Young, Mt. Juliet merchant who assisted in the investigation, and warrant charging young Still with arson on two counts was issued by Magistrate W. H. Conatser.

The Stills moved to Mt. Juliet only a few months ago, and live just across the road from the burned school building.

Discovery that the Stills had suffered from two fires in the past—their home in Nashville and their chicken house in Mt. Juliet had both been burned—caused the officer to question the boy, who had been at home alone on both occasions.

While Williams admitted setting fire to the school and the church, he insisted he had nothing to do with the fires at his home.

In the confession, he said that on the night the school burned (October 23) he arose about two or three o'clock, went to the kitchen of his home and got a few matches, and went over across the road to the school.

"I pushed up a window and climb-
(Continued on Page 5)

Confession Ends

(Continued from Page 1)
ed in," he continued. "I got some paper that was lying around and put it in the corner and set it on fire."

After starting the fire, he said he climbed out of the window and went back and to bed.

The church fire, he said, was started in a similar manner around 6 o'clock Thursday night, by igniting a curtain that hung between two rooms of the church.

He could give no reason for his acts other than that the fires satisfied an uncontrollable desire.

Sgt. Williams and Patrolman Craig asked that the $1,500 reward offered by the people of Mt. Juliet and the additional $100 offered by Sheriff Atkinson for the solution of the case be divided between the funds for rebuilding the school and the church, $800 for each fund.

M. M. Prowell, who joined county and state officers in the investigation, stated that he also wished to contribute to the rebuilding funds.

Earlier major fires in the community had destroyed the Baptist church in March, 1938; the elementary school in February, 1942; the post office in March, 1942; the high school October 23, 1946. Three of these fires struck directly at the school system, since five elementary grades were housed in the Baptist church since the school's burning four years ago.

The 100 pupils in four of the grades which lost their temporary home have resumed classes at the Green Hill Church of Christ. The other grade is being taught at the Mt. Juliet Church of Christ.

Confession Ends

(Continued from Page 5)

The church fire was discovered at about 6 o'clock Thursday night, and the first flames were said to have been observed in the auditorium section of the building, although not directly over the furnace. A bucket brigade, formed immediately was soon backed by trucks from the Lebanon and Nashville fire departments, but the blaze was out of control when the equipment arrived.

Damage to the two-story brick veneer church, rebuilt eight years ago , was estimated at over $35.000, only partially covered by insurance. Loss of kitchen equipment recently installed by the Men's civic club and school equipment increased the damage about $2,000,.

Bloodhounds brought from the state prison by investigators Friday morning failed to find any suspicious trail. A delegation from Mt. Juliet, composed of J. S. Hatfield the Rev. O. L. Rives, pastor of the Baptist church, and Tom Browning, visited Governor Jim McCord Friday and requested state aid in tracking down the arsonist.

The following article is another example of how the Mt. Juliet Baptist Church congregation adapted to the loss of their church. Rev. Rives and his family moved to the second floor of the parsonage so the downstairs rooms could be used for church services. The Parsonage mentioned in this article was later the Mt. Juliet Funeral Home. *Lebanon Democrat December 9, 1946*

Church Congregation Makes Arrangements For Regular Services

The congregation of the Mt. Juliet Baptist church will hold all regular sevices in the parsonage until its building, destroyed by fire, can be reconstructed, it has been announced. The parsonage, a large colonial home formerly owned by the late S. H. Smith, was purchased this summer.

In this emergency, the Rev. O. L. Rives, and family have moved upstairs, making the large downstairs rooms which open together available for the Sunday morning and evening preaching services, the midweek prayer service, the Sunday evening Training Union meeting, and the Cradle Roll, Beginner, Primary, and Adult department of the Sunday School. The Young People's department will meet in the home of Mr. and Mrs. J. A. Gifford; the intermediate department will meet in the home of Mr. and Mrs. J. H. McCorkle; and the junior department will meet in the Masonic lodge hall.

While the church buildings of the community and the surrounding area were offered for use by their congregations, it was decided to utilize the parsonage instead. Several gifts to help with building a new house of worship have been received.

If you're from Mt. Juliet, you'll enjoy this article since it includes a familiar list of folks who contributed to the equipment fund for the new school. A $10 contribution in 1946 would be over $130.00 in 2020 dollars. *Lebanon Democrat, Thursday, December 9, 1946*

Equipment Fund Of Mt. Juliet Schools Receives Over $1000

Contributions to the Mt. Juliet school equipment fund swelled the growing total by over $1000 during the past two weeks, according to announcement of the treasurer. This fund will be used to purchase equipment for the high and elementary schools of Mt. Juliet, which lost all equipment in the recent fires, and the balance, if any, will be turned over to the building fund, the sponsors state.

Contributions received since last publication are as follows:

D. E. Deweese, $10; H. J. Grimes Co., $10; Miss Calhoun, $1; Aaron Twest, $1; Davis Codra, $5; Miss Cathy, $1; Lt. Emmett Franklin, $5; Sam Lyons, $5; Tom Cathcart, $5; Robert Fuqua, $10; C. J. Potter, $10; Howard Tomlinson, $10; A. R. Tomlinson, $50; Mrs. Percy Carver, $5; C. B. Smith, $100; Harris Earhart, $10; Iva Nell Smith, $20; W. B. Jennings, $75; David Hudson, $5; Mrs. Lula King, $1; W. E. Andrews, $5; Mr. Wauford, $1; Mr. Petty, $1; Robert Bradshaw, $10; Helen Curd, $10; Eugene Yelton, $5; Garett Ozment, $10; Jim Sullivan, $15; Miss Ersy Young, $5; M. E. Castleman, $25; John Everette, $50; C. E. Jordon, $25; Mrs. Claude Hardaway, $5; Herbert Talbot, $10; Jo Hunt, $5; Mizell Smith, $25; Mark Garrett, $50; Agnes Lee Garrett, $25; Dollie and Kate Garrett, $25; Joyce Rummage, $5; Mrs. R. J. Bradshaw, $5; J. H. Adams, $25; Mrs. Kate George, $5; Rev. Willoughby, $50; John Riggan, $25; J. C. Spence, $100; W. H. Rice, $25; Sim' Adamson, $15; Mr. Mills, $35; B. C. Hackney, $25; T. J. Browning, $20; N. M. Locke $25.

Sentencing of Still - *Lebanon Democrat December 26, 1946*
  This article presents the sad outcome for the young Still boy..

Boy Arsonist Is Sent to State Home For Feeble Minded

William Wilson Still, 18-year-old Mt. Juliet boy, was found guilty Thursday morning of burning the Mt. Juliet high school building and the Baptist church and was sentenced to serve not less than two nor more than ten years in the state penitentiary for each of the offenses.

Judge John Mitchell will recomment to the warden and the state commissioner of institutions that he be confined in the State Home for the Feeble Minded.

The verdict was reached by agreement between the defense counsel and the attorney-general and the jury accepted the agreement.

The court read a sanity report from Central State Hospital, where Still was examined, and the report stated that the boy was mentally deficient, with the mentality of a nine-year-old child. It added that although he was not insane and knew right from wrong he had a definite trend toward pyromania and was subject to impulses to burn things. The report also stated that he was quiet and well behaved during his stay at the hospital.

The doctors advised that he be confined to the Home for the Feeble Minded for the greatest protection to society.

Four witnesses testified for the state: Sheriff Ewing Atkinson, State Deputy Fire Marshal Kirk Webb, and Highway Patrolmen Bill Williams and Elmer Craig. All told of the investigation that followed the destructive fires and of the Stil boy's voluntary confession when he was accused at his home.

Willard Hagan represented the state and Thomas Hinson was defense attorney.

Mt. Juliet Golden Leaf Yearbook 1946-1947

Charlie Weston authored the class history page for the *Mt. Juliet Golden Leaf* for the 1946-1947 school year and described some of the feelings connected with the loss of the Mt. Juliet High School. An excerpt from that page is shown below.

> *"After we had been in school only seven weeks we were faced with a great disaster. We arose Wednesday morning October 23, 1946, only to hear over the radio that there would be no school at Mt. Juliet that day or the remainder of the week, for at about 2:30 a.m. of this same morning the school had been completely destroyed by fire. Some of the students immediately enrolled in other schools but they were very few in number, for the students as a whole were loyal to their Alma Mater even without a school building.*
>
> *When school was once again resumed the High School was held in Cloyd's Presbyterian Church. The conditions were very crowded, but everyone seemed determined to make the most of a bad situation. It was under these circumstances that we have had to finish High School but because of this we have learned all the better to appreciate the good things. We hope that the new building will be ready for the other classes soon".*

A *Golden Leaf* photograph of the Mt Juliet High School shortly after it burned on October 23,1946.

New School Buildings...

The new Mt. Juliet High School (top) and the new Mt. Juliet Elementary School (bottom)l around 1950 (now 2025 North Mt. Juliet Road).

An excerpt from the 1947-1948 yearbook, the Golden Leaf, reads as follows: "In the fall of '47 we entered the door of our new [high] school building as Dignified Seniors."

And a New Church....

Construction of the Mt. Juliet Baptist Church's third building was started on March 27, 1948. The new building (above) was dedicated on December 7, 1952. It's amazing how much this building resembles the one before it. A close look at old photographs is required to discern the difference. Although the steeple has since been removed, the building still stands near the center of Mt. Juliet.

CHAPTER **6**

The Fire Chief

I WAS FIVE years old in 1950 and of course hadn't started to school. On what I remember as a spring day, Daddy and I went to the nearby town of Lebanon. Lebanon is about 15 miles East of Mt. Juliet and to me was a big city at the time. I'm not sure I knew why we were going until we arrived.

The city of Lebanon had given Mt. Juliet an old fire engine as a start toward our volunteer fire department. The local civic organization, the Mt. Juliet Men's Club of which Daddy was a member, had decided fire protection was long overdue.

The town had had its fill of fires during the nine-year period detailed in the previous chapter. The memories of those fires and the town's helpless rural isolation were probably the biggest catalyst in the Fire Department's creation.

Upon arrival in Lebanon, I recall that we went inside a building where a group of men were sitting and chatting. A couple of men were playing checkers. The next thing I knew we were on the highway heading toward Mt. Juliet. The unusual thing was that we were on a fire engine - a 1917 "American LaFrance" Fire engine.

This great machine intrigued me. There was my father, clutching a large wooden steering wheel at the right side of this open cab vehicle. I sat with him to his left on a long, black leather tufted seat that had a peculiar odor (probably moisture had caused this as a result of the open cab). It was a bit scary to a young boy of my size to be perched high up on the seat of this contraption that had no roof or doors.

The motor had a sound about it that I shall never forget. To this day I have never encountered another like it. The sound was a mixture of throaty, quick - slow and determined noises that made a music all its own. Those of us with a strong love for the internal combustion engine could really appreciate it.

Placed conveniently to my left was a siren with a hand crank. Turning this crank was more fun than going to the store with a nickel to buy candy.

Behind my Dad's right shoulder was a large brass bell with a rope attached to the clangor. The rope ran horizontally all the way to the rear platform so those firemen in this location could ring the bell. No doubt, the numerous volunteers were as intrigued with the bell as I was with the hand siren.

Blocking my dad's exit on his right was at least one long wooden ladder and a hook or two attached to long wooden poles.

The large lights (approximately 14" in diameter) were made of brass and in need of shining, as was the rest of the engine.

It had large wooden spoke, solid rubber wheels (at least 30" in diameter in the front and even larger in the rear) and a chain drive, which is almost unheard of for a four-wheel vehicle. The chain drive proved to be one of the weaker points and l recall it breaking on at least one occasion.

Since the town had no public water supply at the time, water for the 500-gallon tank onboard was obtained from the frequently muddy and out of banks creek. In a field just off Mt. Juliet Road and about two hundred feet below the Mt. Juliet Church of Christ there was a natural sloping access to Stoner Creek that made it fairly convenient to fill the tank. To get the water into the tank, a long hose was coupled to the water pump. A large filter on the creek-end of the hose kept large items from being sucked into the tank.

After filling the tank about dark one day Daddy, with me as his sidekick, started to pull away from the creek. Suddenly the chain snapped, probably due to an old chain, rough terrain and a heavy load of water. It was so late in the day that the chain wasn't repaired until the following morning when more light was available. Today armed security guards would have to stand watch all night.

It wasn't long until the Men's Club decided it was time for our fire department to become more modern, so a project was undertaken to raise funds for a better fire engine.

Because Mt. Juliet was in the center of a rural area, there were frequent grass fires on farm terrain that called for a 4-wheel drive, rough terrain type vehicle to make the most remote fire accessible, while at the same time be versatile enough to be used on paved roads.

Since no such fire engine was available within the Club's means it was decided one would be built locally. Daddy either volunteered or was volunteered to head up the project since (1) he was the owner/operator of the town's only auto repair shop, (2) he was the only reason the town had been able to keep the original American LaFrance Fire Engine in running condition and (3) he was "Fire Chief".

So, the Club's first step was to purchase a government surplus "Dodge Power Wagon" truck chassis. It was just four wheels, a truck cab and an empty chassis at the rear. The firefighting equipment was to be built on as funds were raised.

After the purchase of the Dodge truck the Club's funds were all but depleted. So in order to draw attention to the project and raise money it was decided to make a half-time presentation at a Mt. Juliet High School Friday Night football game.

Both the old "LaFrance" and the new "Dodge" were parked on the sidelines the night of the game. It almost seemed both vehicles were anxiously awaiting a drive around the field at half time to show themselves off. A picture of this scene now would be priceless.

When halftime came the two were driven around as someone talked about the needed funds on a crude public address system. The results weren't much to brag about. The total amount raised that evening was $1.00, donated by two men from the town our team was playing. The Club didn't get discouraged. Successful fund raisers were held after that and the money was finally raised to finish the fire truck.

As has been said, the Dodge Power Wagon was, at the time of purchase, exempt of any resemblance to a fire engine. There was a lot to be done, the least of which was to change the color from "Naval Gray" to "Fire Engine Red". The major work ahead included rebuilding the truck's engine and the installation of a fire fighting water pump (for creating water pressure to put out fires as well as creating a suction for drawing water from the town creek), the 500 gallon water tank, reels, hoses, a siren, red lights, hand railings, rear fenders, standing platforms, and of course the name on the door. The work was all done by my father except for some special welding of the rear fenders and standing platforms which was done at no charge by Mr. Porter (a local resident who was an expert welder for the Nashville Bridge Company).

Dual wheels were added at the rear for the added support of a full water tank. The dual wheels made the rear section of the vehicle a good two feet wider than the front. Many a farm gate was to be widened by this unique feature. More often than not, the driver would forget about the engine's wide behind and plunge with vigor through a smaller opening.

Over a period of several months, the work was finally completed with the final touch being the name painted on the cab doors: *(Daddy removed the doors and they were taken to a professional sign painter by Percy Bates and his son Phillip)*.

The number 1 in the upper left-hand corner was no doubt some optimism that Mt. Juliet would eventually have more than one fire engine.

The finished product wasn't your typical streamlined beauty that the city councils of incorporated towns spend hundreds of thousands of dollars on, but in the eyes of my Dad and the men who had worked to raise money for its creation, it was visible pride.

The city of Lebanon and its Fire Department provided some valuable training and fire fighting demonstrations for the Mt. Juliet volunteer firemen.

Outside of some WWII surplus gas masks there was no protective clothing or equipment for the volunteer firemen. Luckily no one was ever injured.

The Dodge Power Wagon was powerful but not fast. Top speed was about 40 mph unless you had a tail wind going down Phillips' Hill.... then maybe 50. Speed was limited by a six-cylinder flat head engine, 4,165 pounds of extra weight from 500 gallons of water and all the other fire fighting apparatus.

Although I was never at a Men's Club meeting to hear if he received any recognition or praise for his efforts, I feel whatever was said or done was inadequate for all the hours he contributed at no charge. Of course, he didn't do it out of a desire for attention or recognition. It was more because of his love for the automotive trade and his desire to see the town's dream come true. It was an even greater accomplishment for him than it was for the town.

One Sunday afternoon, when I was still a little too young to go to fires, there was a phone call, a few quick words to my Mother about a fire, and my Dad and older brother Richard were out the door. I raced to one of the large front windows and watched with my Mother as our '46 Mercury rounded a curve on two wheels, on the gravel road in front of our house that led to the fire hall. Mother fearfully said, "They'll get killed". They didn't of course. The scene made me excited about my participation in the years to come.

By the time I was 15 and for several years after I got to drive the fire engine and help put out fires. I thought I was pretty cool driving this macho machine.

For a while we parked it at Castleman's Garage during the day and at our home at night. That way my Dad and I could quickly be available for fire calls from either location.

It was an honor to have been a young volunteer fireman and it has made me admire all first responders in our country!

I wrote "The Fire Chief" as an early 68ᵗʰ birthday present for Daddy and gave it to him October 16, 1978.

Fire Engine Given To Mt. Juliet Community By City of Lebanon

Citification of Mt. Juliet continues apace, with the addition of a fire engine, which was contributed by the city of Lebanon recently. The engine was the 1917 model American-LaFrance, and had not been used here in fighting fires for the past several years, but was still in excellent condition, it is s ted.

A water tank was placed on the engine by M. E. Castleman and Elwin Weston after its delivery to Mt. Juliet. The tank will hold sufficient water to meet the demands of any average fire, according to information given by Lebanon Fire Chief Dallas Young to the Mt. Juliet firefighters.

A demonstration was given recently following a meeting of the Mt. Juliet Men's club, when a fire was started in the school grounds, and proper fire-fighting methods were demonstrated by Chief Young. Mayor William D. Baird of Lebanon, whose interest made the gift possible, and Chief Young were guests of the club at dinner.

Funds for operation and maintenance of the fire engine are contributed by the business men of the community, and J. A. Gifford is serving as treasurer for the group.

Street lights were recently installed in the community, with the cost being met by voluntary subscription of the business men.

Mt. Juliet volunteer fire fighters will attend the fire fighting institute to be held this spring at Murfreesboro, at the invitation of Mayor Baird and Chief Young.

Lebanon Democrat Thursday, March 2, 1950 (Front Page)

An early photo of the 1917 American LaFrance fire engine purchased new by the city of Lebanon for $850.00. (photo courtesy of Chief Henry Preston, Lebanon Fire Department)

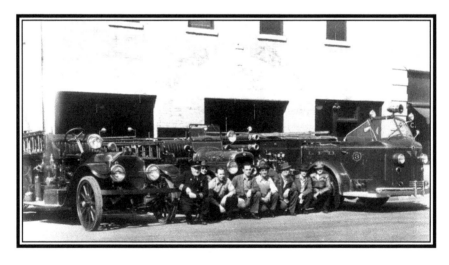

Lebanon firefighters pose in front of their oldest to newest fire engines. This photo was made not too long before Lebanon gave their 1917 American LaFrance (left) to Mt. Juliet. (photo courtesy of Chief Henry Preston, Lebanon Fire Department –circa 1949).

"Dude" Hibbett, one of the many volunteer firemen, poses at the wheel (right hand drive) of the 1917 "LaFrance" Fire Engine. Note the wood spoke wheels and solid rubber tires.

Our Model "A" Ford Truck can barely be seen on the right as it cools under the big shade tree outside Castleman's Garage. On hot summer days Daddy would sometimes repair autos under this tree instead of inside. Also, some folks wanted to do their own repairs and ask Daddy for free advice. Usually they ended up under this tree and became true "shade tree mechanics".

(photo taken around 1950)

One of the first fires to be put out by the Mt. Juliet Volunteer Fire Department.

Station Burns At Mt. Juliet

The Mt. Juliet Volunteer Fire Department put out a large fire Monday night at McFarlands Service Center and saved the building despite the loss of several thousand dollars worth of stock.

Buck Holland was on his way home from work at 2 a.m. and heard some shots. He looked in the direction of the noise to see smoke rising Then he investigated, got to a phone, called the operator about the fire, and she notified the fire department.

After the fire he discovered the noise he had heard was several shotgun shells exploding from the heat. Also after the fire there were several batteries in one corner with the caps popped off.

The operator who was on duty at the time told officials that she had gotten her signal from the number McFarland's about an hour before Mr. Holland reported the fire.

Macon Castleman is chief of the department and was assisted at the flood light by N. C. Hibbett.

According to Chief Castleman the origin of the fire was undetermined, but damage was about half covered by insurance.

Donelson Diary, August 31, 1950

Ready for a fire!

Formally a Dodge Power Wagon truck chassis, now the new fire engine for the Mt. Juliet Volunteer Fire Department. This photo was probably taken around 1951 or 1952 and represents the great end result of hundreds of man-hours my Dad put into this project. Note the front bumper was re-configured around the large protruding fire fighting water pump that was adapted to the front of the engine.

(In the upper left corner you can see a late 30's model coupe parked beside the barbershop and the red Pegasus horse on the Mobil Oil sign at Tomlinson's Store.)

"Coming and going". Two good photos of the new fire engine. I enjoy the background in these shots as much as the subject. At the right in the bottom photo you can almost read "MT. JULIET" on the end of the little three-walled passenger shelter that belonged to the Tennessee Central Railroad.

CHAPTER 7

First Call to Breakfast

Background.

My Mother, Katherine Elizabeth Carver, was born March 28, 1912. Exactly twelve days before her 12th birthday her Mother, Evie Inez Carver, passed away at the young age of 36 due to heart problems. She left a 35-year-old husband, Henry Gilliam Carver, and 10 children between the ages of 5 weeks and 15 years.

The family depended on its 100-acre farm for 100% of its food, clothing and shelter. All of the children who were old enough worked on the farm by helping tend the crops and care for the livestock.

While Mother always did her part and helped out with the regular farm chores, someone had to prepare meals for the family. Even though she was the second oldest daughter, she was the one who began cooking three meals a day for a family of 11 at the age of 11. Planning and cooking even one meal for a family this big must have been overwhelming for a little girl. However, as the short story below describes, Mother was smart, organized, efficient and confident. While I think she was born with these fine qualities, they probably had to develop at light speed necessity during that spring of 1924.

Her family and friends fondly remember and still talk about what a great cook she was. When someone complimented her cooking she would respond in a humble and reserved tone by saying, "it does very well". If you went on and on about it you might have gotten an, "I'm glad you enjoyed it" and her warm smile. Her exceptionally good cooking was just one of the many things that made her such a wonderful Mother.

I would be sound asleep. Then suddenly I was awakened to the metallic clanking noise a skillet makes when jerked from the middle of a pile of pots and pans. This familiar sound was only part of our morning reveille. The brief symphony was enhanced by the added tone of the orchestra's echo chamber…the bottom drawer of our all metal, Norge electric range.

Mother made no effort to do her pre-cooking work quietly. It's as if on some level she knew she was the family's alarm clock.

Following the abrupt start of our daily kitchen sonata (perhaps it really sounded more like a train wreck) there would be a brief moment of quiet when we would drift back into our comfortable slumber. This wouldn't last long because the next part of the symphony would begin with the very soft sounds bacon and sausage make as they begin their sizzle. As the heat at the bottom of the skillet increased so did the hissing sound until the frying reached a sustained peak. Making this part of the music even more irresistible was the added dimension of smell - an instant appetizer that made you want to get out of bed and find the source.

My frequent visits to the kitchen at about this point in the morning always found Mother completely dressed and ready for the day. Often I would arrive just as she was beginning one of the many things she did so exceptionally well…making homemade biscuits.

To the right of the stove was the beginning of our white enamel, Youngstown metal cabinets. A few pieces of the cabinetry were purchased and used from 1949 to 1952 while we lived in our garage home one level below. These originals, along with some new additions, made up the "L" shaped cabinet arrangement that connected the space between the stove and refrigerator.

The cabinet immediately next to the stove had a flour sifter built into the upper cabinet. The sifter held five pounds of flour and was pulled out on tracks over the counter below. A drawer in the lower cabinet held a white baker's cloth, rolling pin and biscuit cutter.

Mother would spread the baker's cloth on the flat cabinet surface and lay the rolling pin and biscuit cutter to one side. Next, she would open the two upper cabinet doors and pull the sifter out over the baker's cloth.

With fluid motion she would remove the cap on the bottom of the sifter with her left hand and turn the crank with her right. After just enough sifted flour fell to the surface below, lard, milk, flour, salt and baking powder or soda were added. With her hands she would mix and knead the dough into a large mound. Next came several quick passes of the rolling pin and finally the biscuit cutter. She wasted no time and there was no lost motion. It all seemed to be so natural for her.

She carefully placed each cut out biscuit on a large cookie sheet. The cookie sheet filled to capacity was then placed in her pre-heated oven.

Next the table would be set (I was quickly taught how, as a result of standing around in the way). A butter dish with a stick of real butter would be placed in front of my Dad's plate. Another butter dish with a stick of oleo was placed in the middle of the table for the rest of us. The butter wasn't off limits to anyone, but it was sort of discouraged by its proximity. Along with the butter and oleo was an array of Mother's homemade jams and jellies as well as sorghum molasses some friend of the family always seemed to be giving us. And…how well I remember Mother using an ice pick to make two small opposing holes in the top of a small can of *Carnation Evaporated Milk*. Our table wasn't set unless that can was in front of Daddy's plate so he could lighten up his morning cup of coffee.

Soon after the biscuit baking began, the bacon and sausage frying would be finished. Most of the grease would be emptied from the frying pan into a grease cup that sat in the middle space between the four burners on the top of the stove. The grease cup had sort of a brushed aluminum appearance and had the words "Grease" imprinted on its side. It was part of a matching canister set that was popular for that day. A small portion of the grease would be intentionally left in the skillet and used for scrambling eggs. Mother's right hand exerted just the right amount of pressure to crack each egg on the side of the skillet, and then both hands were used to quickly and neatly dump the contents. The yokes and whites were blended in the skillet during the scrambling process. Somehow that skillet was always at just the right temperature because the scrambled eggs were always perfect.

As the perfectly baked hot biscuits were removed from the oven, Mother would call us to the table. One of us would say the blessing and the seven of us would enjoy the food and time together. Usually there would be very little food left over. If any of the 18 biscuits and other food wasn't eaten it would be placed in the center of the kitchen table and eaten as a mid-morning snack. After that it became a main course for Nappy, our favorite dog.

That was it. That was breakfast at our house in 1952. It was all prepared in just a few minutes and consumed in even less. I can still hear, smell and taste all of it. Especially those wonderful biscuits!

In early August of 1997 I asked Mother to give me her biscuit recipe while I wrote, and this is how it went:

Mother's Biscuits
Lard (amount that fits in the palm of your hand – about a tablespoon)
2 cups of flour
1 teaspoon of soda
2 teaspoons of baking powder
½ cup buttermilk (use soda and baking powder)
or
½ cup sweet milk (use baking powder only)
Roll out thin so biscuits are not too fluffy (your Daddy liked "hard tacks")
Makes 16-18 biscuits

Mother dressed up and on her way to church. This was probably about 9:45 AM. By this time she had fixed a huge breakfast for seven, cleaned up the kitchen and started Sunday dinner (lunch).

This photo was taken some time between 1952 and 1955. I don't think the blocks were painted until after that time period.

CHAPTER 8

Radio and Picture Shows

PRIOR TO AND during the better part of 1950, entertainment was mostly the radio and an occasional movie or what we then called a picture show.

The radio seemed to be on all the time at my house and at Castleman's Garage. I have fond memories of what seemed to be an endless supply of very entertaining radio shows.

Having sound as the only dimension made the programs even better because you were forced to use the imagination of your mind's eye. It was wonderful to visualize what the characters were doing as you heard their voices and the sound effects. Radio in those days was a lot like reading a book.

Most programs lasted only 15 minutes, which is about the length of most people's attention span. Some of my favorite shows included, "Baby Snooks", "Mr. and Mrs. North", "Gangbusters", "The Inner Sanctum", "The Green Hornet", "Sky King", "Don McNeil's Breakfast Club" (*first call to breakfast*), "Lets Pretend with Little Orly", "Sergeant Preston of the Yukon", "Life with Luigi", and "Fibber McGee and Molly".

Each radio show had its own special introduction or theme song. For example, "The Inner Sanctum" began with the sound of a squeaking door and "Gangbusters" began with the sound of machine gun fire. "Let's Pretend" had a theme song that is unforgettable. "Whispering Streets", "Stella Dallas" and "Young Dr. Malone" were shows I remember but didn't enjoy or make a point to follow because they were intended for an older audience. Someone in our household must have enjoyed them because the frequency of their intros is indelibly inscribed in my memory.

Born in January of 1945, I've discovered I'm actually pretty young to remember the old radio shows that were on prior to television. When I wax nostalgic with others my age or even a year or two older, many of them have no memory of this. Perhaps being the youngest of five children made the difference for me. Even then I remember two good shows being on different stations at the same time and big arguments among my siblings as to which one would be heard....would we listen to "Baby Snooks" or "Mr. and Mrs. North"?

Going to the picture show was a special treat in 1950 and usually only happened on Saturday night. The Donelson Theater was the one most frequented by my family, but The Capitol and Princess Theaters in Lebanon were often patronized as well. At age 5 the best part of the picture show for me was the cartoon during which time we were allowed to sit on the front edge of the theater seat in the up position so big people didn't block your view. One of the first films I remember seeing in a theater was "Ma and Pa Kettle Go To Town", which came out in 1950.

As I got older and could go to the movies on my own, I learned to love the great movie houses in Nashville. The Tennessee, Loews' and The Paramount, all on Church Street, were among my favorites and each had its own character.

Just off Church Street was the Knickerbocker. Unique in design, it had two ticket windows making it possible to enter from either end. The traditional "screen in front of you" entrance was on 6th Avenue. If you bought your ticket on the Capitol Boulevard side, you had the unusual experience of entering from behind the screen.

There's something about the ambience of seeing a film in a dark theater, being part of an audience's reaction and eating popcorn that's magic to me. Watching a movie at home on TV is no match for the big silver screen.

As long as I can remember I've loved going to the movies. On average, I've been a patron once a week most of my life. To this day it remains one of my favorite things to do.

Grand opening night of the Tennessee Theatre on Church Street in downtown Nashville on February 28, 1952. You can barely make out the vertical Paramount sign further down Church Street. (courtesy of the Nashville Public Library -Special Digital Collection)

CHAPTER 9

Friday Night Live

DURING MY TWELVE years of school, from 1951 through 1963, the Mt. Juliet School Auditorium was located in the grammar school building (2025 North Mt. Juliet Road) and it served all 12 grades. It was a focal point of our school and community - an exciting gathering place for many events: student assemblies, graduation exercises, PTA and community meetings, 16mm movies, and assorted live performances.

Like many school structures it was designed to handle more than one function. While it was primarily an auditorium, it also served as the cafeteria for the elementary school as well as the high school located about one hundred feet to the north. The stage was used as the dining area and the kitchen was located stage left. Folding tables and chairs in the dining area were in a constant state of being put away so the stage could be used or put back in place prior to the next lunch time meal.

I don't know how many people the auditorium would seat. If I had to guess, the main floor would hold 400 or so and the balcony another hundred. The main floor seats were wooden folding chairs with padded seats...actually fairly comfortable. The balcony seating consisted of small four-legged stools. While the floor downstairs was concrete and flat, the balcony floor was wooden and elevated via long stepped platforms that led upward to short windows which provided an occasional escape to the roof above the elementary school hallway. A balcony seat was especially coveted by young boys and as a result became a haven for mischief and raucous behavior that was usually accompanied by an inordinate amount of noise from the wooden floor.

1. Mt. Juliet School Auditorium; 2. Mt. Juliet Elementary School; 3. Mt. Juliet High School; 4. Mt. Juliet High School Gymnasium; 5. Mt. Juliet School Cafeteria and covered walkway to connect the two buildings were added after the 1954-1955 school year.

Movies

I used to love going to the school sponsored movies that were shown in the auditorium. It seems like we got to do this more than we deserved, but no one objected. The movie would usually start late in the afternoon and finish just in time for the buses to leave for home. The shades on the tall auditorium windows would be lowered to block the daylight while a high school student would thread the film through an old 16mm sound projector. Each movie began with the crowd counting backwards in unison as the leader on the film exposed production countdown numbers. Unfortunately the film was constantly breaking, or the sound was not synchronized with the picture but we didn't mind. How could we complain, we were not in class and since there was no movie theater in Mt. Juliet this was the only movie-going opportunity for many of the students.

Most of the movies were Westerns but I also remember seeing films with more educational value such as *The Grapes of Wrath*.

One of the old 16-mm projectors used by the school back then came into my possession and I've since passed it on to my son Joe. According to Richard, it was an old W.W. II Army surplus model that he used when he was one of the school's projectionists. I too, was a projectionist in high school and when I graduated, the principal, Mr. Higgins, gave the old projector to me at the end of my senior year. At that time it had been years since it had been used because the school had purchased a new one.

Along with the projector came an old 16mm newsreel from Castle Films that is circa late 40's or early 50's. These newsreels used to come along with and be shown before the movies that the school rented. Somewhere along the way our family began to watch this film on at least an annual basis – often after all the presents were opened on Christmas Day. We called it the "Alligator Movie" because it's about alligator hunting in Burma. I converted it to video a few years ago and put a little Christmas message from me at the beginning, then had copies made to give everyone in the family. They were all really surprised because the projector had been broken for many years and they had all forgotten about it. I still watch it every now and then and it never fails to make me feel like I'm back in that old auditorium.

Plays

While I treasure all of the memories of the events that took place in the old auditorium, plays are at the top of my list. One of my first recollections happened during the 1949–1950 school year – probably in the spring of 1950. This was the year prior to my first year of school in which I wandered around the school building and made a nuisance of myself while my Mother worked in the school cafeteria. Since a lot of my time was spent near the cafeteria, I remember watching high school boys construct and paint the walls of the set that were made of canvas stretched over tall wooden frames. No doubt someone explained to me what was going on, but it became even clearer once the walls were placed in front of the beige backdrop curtains and fastened together to make an artificial room on the stage. All this fascinated me.

In the late spring of 1955 I went to see Richard and Evalena in their Senior and Junior Class Plays respectively. No one had to twist my arm to go. It was exciting to imagine what characters my big brother and sister would portray. Before the big night, I remember fellow students from their classes coming to our classroom with a diagram of the seating in the auditorium drawn on something like a large piece of poster board. They were selling advance tickets and I assume all seats were reserved or at least assigned on a first come, first assigned basis.

On the nights their plays took place, my eyes were glued to the footlights on that old stage, waiting for those huge maroon curtains to open and draw me into the story. When it finally did, the first things that caught my eye were the walls they had made for the set, the location of the fake doors and windows and how the furniture was arranged. It was so exciting to see people I knew and looked up to in different character. The makeup those teenagers wore to make themselves look like middle age adults intrigued me. I became totally focused on what was happening on stage and forgot everything else.

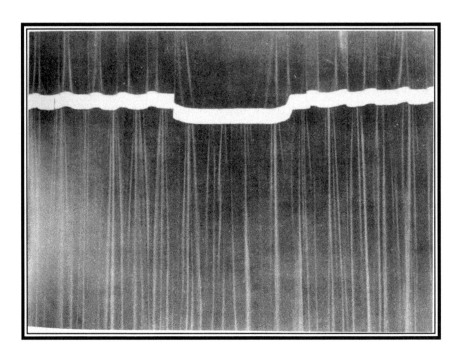

The big maroon stage curtains in the Mt. Juliet School Auditorium.

It seems most plays were scheduled on Friday nights. A few of the play programs from those years support this:

Those Darling Brats
A Three Act Comedy, Presented by the Senior Class, Friday April 30, 1954, 8:00 PM

Father Knows Best
A Three Act Comedy, Presented by the Senior Class, Friday, March 11, 1955, 7:30 PM

Headin' For a Weddin'
A Three Act Hillbilly Comedy, Presented by the Junior Class, Friday, April 8, 1955, 8:00 PM

Marriage "Wows, Life O' The Party and Wilbur's Wild Night
Three One Act Comedies, Presented by the Senior Class, Friday, April 6, 1956, 7:30 PM

The Ole District School
Two Acts, Presented by the Mt. Juliet Men's Club, Friday, June 17, 1955, 8:00 PM

Junior and Senior plays were also presented during school hours the following week and even though I went with my parents on Friday night I attended these as well. They were every bit as good the second time.

From all those early memories I became hooked and knew I wanted to be in my own Junior and Senior Plays. Unfortunately this was not to happen. Because of so much growth in student enrollment, the Mt. Juliet Elementary School ran out of room, so the auditorium was divided into four classrooms. How could this happen right on the eve of my Junior year? How, after waiting so long, could I and my classmates be denied our big night as amateur actors, how could all my older siblings get to do this and not I and how could this "right of passage" possibly be taken away?

This was a big disappointment that stayed with me for many years. It wasn't until I wrote and reflected on the chapter entitled "Scrapbook of Nine Fiery Years" that I finally put it into perspective. I realize now that my junior and senior years were not the first time there was no auditorium in which to have a play. For example, the junior and senior classes of 1946-1947 experienced an even greater deprivation as a result of the loss of their entire school building in October of 1946.

The cast and stage crew for "Father Knows Best", presented by the Senior Class of 1955. Seated from the left, Sylvia McCFarland, Nancy Corley, Linda McCorkle, Sandra Potter, Babs Foster, Richard Castleman, Onita Jackson. Standing from the left, Aline Brown, Wendall Harris, Brigger Pike, Donnie Eakes, Lon Mires, James Carter Martin, Aline Fields, Bonnie Vantrease and Mrs. Clyde Taylor. Note: Sylvia McFarland is seated in one of the auditorium's folding wooden chairs.

*Some of "The Ole District School" cast members posing for the camera. From the left, Jack Gifford, Joe Falkner, Macon Castleman, Humphrey McCorkle and Travis Garrett. (*Two Acts, Presented by the Mt. Juliet Men's Club, Friday, June 17, 1955, 8:00 PM)

A scene from "The Ole District School". From the left, Jack Gifford, Travis Garrett, Mildred McCorkle, Hilton Tubb, Humphrey McCorkle, unknown, unknown, and Riley Butler.

CHAPTER **10**

Getting Ready for Television

SOMETIME AROUND 1947, Daddy expanded his auto repair business to include the sale, installation and repair of Norge stoves, refrigerators and washers and Zenith radios. The small inventory of appliances for this sideline to his regular business was made possible via a business loan arranged through the Bank of Mt. Juliet.

Braid Electric Company, which was located on Demombreum Street at 8th Avenue in Nashville, was his single source wholesale supplier. I remember Richard and me going to Braid's with him to pick up items in our Model A Ford truck. On one of these trips I recall it being the first time to notice Daddy whistling a tune and watching his cheeks sort of flutter as he bent the notes. I also recall the two-piece hood on the truck would not fasten down good on either side, so it flew up like wings as we sped west on highway 70 to Nashville. *(more about this beloved Model A Ford Truck in Chapter 12)*.

One afternoon in early 1950, I remember going to Castleman's Garage where Daddy was in the process of painting a dark red semi-circle on the shop floor near the office in the corner. He had also begun outlining a yellow border about 8 inches wide on the outer edge of the semi-circle. Since my sister Evalena was artistic he handed her a paintbrush and asked her to help with the tedious work of painting the yellow border. The semi-circle stood out from the rest of Dad's garage. After the bright semi-circle dried Daddy used it as a small showroom to better merchandise the Norge and Zenith Products.

What I didn't know then was that the real motivation behind

the painting of the semi-circle was to showcase the coming of one of the most revolutionary consumer products ever known to man… Television.

WSM-TV, an NBC affiliate, would become Nashville's first TV station with a projected airdate of Saturday, September 30, 1950. Sometime before this date Daddy began selling Zenith TV's in addition to the other appliances. Actually we had only one or two TV's in inventory at first.

Well in advance of the historic Saturday, Daddy erected a tall TV antenna on top of Castleman's Garage that could be seen from all over Mt. Juliet. I'm guessing the antenna mast must have been 35-40 feet in overall length since the garage had a 20-foot ceiling and the bottom of the antenna came within 6 feet of the garage floor. It had an L shaped handle at the bottom of the mast so it could easily be turned in any direction for better reception. Before WSM's airdate he would try to get reception on the screen. I remember several attempts accompanied by a very snowy and faint picture and I would hear him say something like, "I think that's Memphis".

My sister Bettye reminded me that Gloria McFarland's dad, "Toppie", also had a TV before there was a station in Nashville and that he could pick up Atlanta and Memphis. I vaguely remember Toppie having a very tall antenna outside his house in Mt. Juliet (when he lived across Mt. Juliet Road from was is now the location of the Mt. Juliet Public Library) …it was about the height of our school's flagpole.

I'd often wondered which stations and from what cities we might have been receiving a faint signal before Nashville's September 30, 1950 debut. A little research revealed several possibilities in addition to Memphis....

AIR DATE	CITY	CALL LETTERS	AFFILIATE	CHANNEL
September 29, 1948	Atlanta	WSB-TV	ABC	
November 24, 1948	Louisville	WAVE-TV	NBC	Channel 3
December 11, 1948	Memphis	WMC-TV	NBC	
July 4, 1949	Birmingham	WBRC-TV		Channel 6
March 6, 1950	Lousiville	WHAS-TV		Channel 11
September 30, 1950	*Nashville*	*WSM-TV*	*NBC*	*Channel 4*

Following are two examples of Daddy's appliance advertising in the Donelson Diary before Television.

Donelson Diary January 9, 1947

Donelson Diary, May 5, 1947

CHAPTER **11**

TV Finally Arrives

BEGINNING IN 1929 and continuing through the early 1950's, the Mt. Juliet Chapter of the Future Farmers of America sponsored a community fair each fall at the Mt. Juliet High School. These fairs had all kinds of events, contests and exhibits including poultry, dairy cows, sheep, hay, small grain, tobacco, corn, fruits and vegetables, home canning, home cooking, home art, a baby show and a horse show. In addition, local merchants were allowed to exhibit their latest merchandise in hopes that it would bring in new customers.

It was fortuitous that the second day of the 1950 fair, Saturday, September 30, 1950, was conveniently timed with WSM-TV's first day of telecasting.

Program cover for the 1950 Mt. Juliet Community Fair

Daddy seized the opportunity to advertise that he was selling TV's by having at least one Zenith TV on display in the high school gymnasium. Braid Electric helped with the effort by supplying him with some cardboard tradeshow displays and brochures that told all about the new Zenith TV.

Although I remember Daddy setting up the display and hooking up the TV in the southeast corner of the high school gym floor, I don't remember the precise moment the first ever TV signal was received from WSM. But I've been told it was there in the gym on that Saturday at 1:10 PM.

Daddy's efforts paid off. Charles "Hooty" Smith, owner of Smith's Rolling Stores and our next-door neighbor, said he was so taken with seeing a TV for the first time at the fair that he had to have one. He called Daddy the following Monday and immediately ordered one to be delivered as soon as possible. J.C. "Fergie" Ferguson told me he had the same experience as "Hooty".

One of the first TV programs I remember was The Camel News Caravan with John Cameron Swayze (years later he became known for saying "It takes a licking but keeps on ticking" in Timex watch commercials). For 15 minutes every Monday through Friday night Swayze simply read the news to the TV audience from typewritten pages. As the name implies, Camel Cigarettes sponsored this early NBC news program. Other early shows included Kukla, Fran and Ollie, Howdy Doody and The Stu Erwin Show a.k.a. The Trouble with Father. Although Stu Erwin was filmed, almost all other programs were live especially local shows. David Cobb and Dave Overton were local WSM personalities from day one.

During TV's first few weeks more people than usual came to Castleman's Garage. As a result, lots of chairs were moved onto the little showroom floor and lined up, theater style, in front of the TV. People we normally didn't see very often became our best friends and would camp out for hours. It became common place for people of all ages to watch the TV test pattern for long periods of time while waiting for the first program of the day to come on the air.

Mr. and Mrs. Sam Jordan (she ran the school cafeteria and he ran Jordan's Grocery Store) also were among the first folks in Mt. Juliet to have a TV (which I'm pretty sure my Dad sold to them). People would just show up at their house unannounced and hang out in their living room in front of their TV. Everyone in Mt. Juliet was welcome at Daddy's garage showroom or the Jordan's living room.

At this time we were living in our garage-home (see The Blockhouse – Chapter 4). Even though Daddy sold TV's we didn't have one at home during this period...at least not full time. Since Castleman's Garage was closed only on Sunday, at the close of business on Saturday Daddy would remove a TV from the showroom floor and load it in the back of our Model-A Ford Truck and bring it home. The TV was placed on Mother's sewing machine cabinet in our already overcrowded front room.

On Saturday nights we all enjoyed watching "Your Show of Shows" with Sid Caesar, Imogene Coca, Carl Reiner and Howard Morris. On Sunday evenings we never missed "The Colgate Comedy Hour" which included a variety of hosts including, Eddie Cantor, Abbott &

Costella, Martin and Lewis, etc.

It was an absolute thrill to see my Dad and my older brother Richard move the TV into the front room on Saturday night but depressing to see it leave early Monday morning so it could be returned to the small showroom floor at Castleman's Garage. Finally, one Monday he left the TV at home and we had it all the time. Having a TV was a real luxury that early in the era and I don't think I ever took it for granted.

As I look back to 1950 when WSM-Channel 4 was the only station and compare it to the multitude of channels available on cable today I can truthfully say that you can have too much of a good thing. Turning the TV on today and surfing many hundreds of channels is totally unexciting. Tuning into one channel with a snowy black & white picture on a small round screen was an awesome experience I wish could be put into words.

	WSM-TV—CHANNEL 4	
	SATURDAY, SEPTEMBER 30	
Time	Program	Origin
1:10 p.m.	Sign on	(Local)
1:15	TV Parade	(Local)
1:30	Pre-game color	(Du Mont)
1:50	Notre Dame vs. North Carolina	(Du Mont)
4:15	Football Scoreboard	(Du Mont)
4:30	Barber of Seville	(Film)
6:00	To Be Announced	
7:00	Saturday Nite Revue	(NBC)
9:30	To Be Announced	
10:00	Don McNeill's TV Club	(ABC)
11:00	Sign off	
	SUNDAY, OCTOBER 1	
3:30 p.m.	Fred Waring	(CBS)
4:30	Weekly Newsreel	(Film)
4:45	To Be Announced	
5:00	To Be Announced	
5:30	Vanderbilt-Auburn game	(Film)
6:30	To Be Announced	
7:00	Comedy Revue	(NBC)
8:00	Philco Playhouse	(NBC)
9:00	To Be Announced	
9:30	Toast of the Town	(CBS)
10:30	Sign off	

Nashville's first ever TV Program Schedule -
Saturday, September 30 and Sunday, October 1, 1950
Nashville Banner, Saturday, September 30, 1950

Radio And TV

MONDAY—WSM-TV—CHANNEL

1:40 A View of Religion	Live	6:45 News Caravan	NBC-L
1:45 Showroom	NBC-K	7:00 What's My Name	NBC-L
2:00 Miss Susan	NBC-L	7:30 Voice of Firestone	NBC-L
2:15 To Be Announced		8:00 Lights Out	NBC-L
2:30 Bert Parks	NBC-L	8:30 WSM, WSM-TV Ann'sary Show Live
3:00 Kate Smith	NBC-L	9:30 Who Said That	NBC-L
4:00 Hawkins Falls	NBC-L	10:00 Tennessee Jamboree	Live
4:15 The Handyman	Live	10:15 Telenews Sports	Live-F
4:30 Howdy Doody	NBC-L	10:30 Weather Report	Live
5:00 Western Corral	Live-F	10:35 Danger.	CBS-K
6:00 Kukla, Fran & Ollie	NBC-L	11:00 Perry Como	CBS-K
6:30 To Be Announced		11:15 Freddy Martin	NBC-K

TUESDAY—WSM-TV—CHANNEL

1:40 The Quest Book	Live	6:30 Fashions	Live
1:45 Cooking with Katherine	Live	6:45 News Caravan	NBC-L
2:00 Miss Susan	NBC-L	7:00 Star Theatre	NBC-L
2:15 To Be Announced	—	8:00 Fireside Theatre	NBC-K
2:30 Bill Goodwin	NBC-L	8:30 Circle Theatre	NBC-K
3:00 Kate Smith	NBC-L	9:00 Carousel	Live
4:00 Hawkins Falls	NBC-L	9:30 Royal Playhouse	Film
4:15 Women's Supplement.	Live	10:00 Tennessee Jamboree	Live
4:30 Howdy Doody	NBC-L	10:15 Telenews & Sports	Live-F
5:00 Western Corral	Live-F	10:30 Weather Report	Live
6:00 Kukla, Fran & Ollie	NBC-L	10:35 Stu Erwin	ABC-K

WSM's Monday and Tuesday line up of TV programming for
October 2 and 3, 1950.
Nashville Banner, Sunday, October 1, 1950

131

You saw and enjoyed Zenith at your Mt. Juliet Fair . . . Now get Zenith for your own home.

Accept This

ZENITH *Challenge*

Test-View Before You Buy TV. See Zenith's New 2-in-1 Screen...Get Proof of Superiority You'll Enjoy a Lifetime!

Giant Circle Picture

Rectangular Type Picture

Zenith Gives You
TWO Picture Shapes In ONE Set

Make a 15-Minute Screen Test of Zenith side-by-side with any conventional set. See how Zenith's *Giant Circle Screen* lets you see the *details* of baseball, football and other action events large and clear ... by using the entire picture area of the big circular tube, instead of just a part of it!

Then — at the flick of a magic switch — see how Zenith gives you the *Rectangular Type* picture which some folks like for viewing close-ups of titles and studio programs.

Add to this Zenith's amazing *Reflection-Proof* and glare-free viewing ease, and you have the finest picture quality ever known in television! Make the Zenith 15-Minute

Screen Test and see the *proof* before you buy. *Be safe instead of sorry!*

Only Zenith Gives You All These

New "SUPER-RANGE" CHASSIS — for clearer reception especially in weak signal areas . . . new "LAZY BONES" REMOTE CONTROL — lets you change programs from your easy chair (optional in all new Zenith* TV sets) . . . PRE-TUNED PICTUREMAGNET BUILT-IN ANTENNA — needs no adjustments . . . BUILT-IN PROVISION FOR TUNER STRIPS TO RECEIVE THE PROPOSED ULTRA-HIGH FREQUENCIES on present standards . . . GLORIOUS NEW CABINETS of lifetime beauty and quality!

Visit Our Store for an Actual Demonstration

Castleman's Garage

Daddy's newspaper ad six days following TV's debut in the Mt. Juliet High School Gymnasium.
Donelson Diary on October 5, 1950

Christmas Day (Monday, December 25, 1950) in the front room of our two-room garage-home. Left to right: Janice, Evalena, Bettye and me. The overhead garage door is at our backs and we're facing the kitchen area of the room where I assume Mother, Daddy and Richard were standing at the time of the photo. The foot of Mother and Daddy's bed can barely be seen at the left. The Zenith table-model TV was home for the weekend and would be returned to the showroom floor at Castleman's Garage the next morning. You can see the antenna wire that runs up the wall from the back of the TV and across the ceiling to a roof mounted antenna.

This photo puts the 5-foot height and 2-foot thickness of the old school foundation into perspective. The eight-inch thick concrete blocks, which were cemented on the outer edge of the top of the foundation wall, left plenty of shelf room for our telephone, which sits behind the TV.

CHAPTER 12

The "Workhorse" Model A

I LOVED OUR Model A Ford Truck. It had a dull black finish and a flat wooden stake bed over the rear wheels that had no fenders. Old photos show it was part of the family as early as 1945 and we kept it until around 1951. It played a memorable role in my early life and was instrumental in developing my lifelong love and appreciation for trucks and cars. As a very young boy I used to imagine our Model A was one of the trucks in my hand when I played with toy trucks and cars in the dirt.

It wasn't born a truck. I didn't know this until 1997 when Richard mentioned it during one of our waxing nostalgic sessions. It was originally a 1928 or 1929 Model A Ford Passenger car-either a 2 or 4 door sedan. A recent conversation with the President of the Model A Ford Club of America revealed it wasn't all that uncommon for a Model A sedan to be reincarnated as a truck. Model A sedans were plentiful and one of the cheapest cars around. If an owner needed a truck more than a car all it took was a cutting torch to eliminate the body a few inches behind the front doors and a few modifications to make the switch. I'm pretty sure our Model A had been converted before we bought it--at least I don't remember Daddy ever saying he was involved.

It was truly the family "workhorse" and helped put food on our table in a variety of ways. It was used at Castleman's Garage to reach and assist stranded motorists—these were referred to as "road calls". Road calls could occur at any time of the day or night and were often during the worst possible weather. During the time the garage was open -generally 7:30 AM to 6:30 PM every day except Sunday- Daddy would often leave the shop open and unattended when he was on a road call. The phone would often ring at home when the garage was closed as well. Daddy often felt obligated to respond to these after hour calls and it never went over well with Mother.

Road calls came in several varieties. A really sick car would be towed back to the garage with a large log chain. The objective for the driver of the towed car was to pay very close attention to the tension on the chain and not run into the back of the Model A when it slowed down or braked. To make it a little more challenging, our Model A had no rear bumper or brake lights.

Minor problems, like flat tires or dead batteries were fixed on the spot. A jack, lug wrench, air tank and hot battery were usually carried on the bed of the truck in order to be prepared for anything. Some cars that were stubborn about starting with a booster battery would be "pushed off". Pushing a car to start it involved matching the big wood bumper on the front of the Model A with the rear bumper of the stalled car. The owner would be told to put the car in first or second gear and to hold the clutch in until the car was up to 10 to 15 miles an hour and then release the clutch. Many car owners were quite skilled at knowing what to do and when, while others never seemed to get the hang of it. Some folks in the latter category would be pushed a mile or two without being able to start their car. Daddy would finally stop pushing, get out of the truck and walk forward to the driver's door. He would then say something like, "you do have the ignition switch on, don't you?". This was usually the right question to ask and the answer was often not the one he wanted to hear—something like, "oh, does the switch have to be on?" A little thing like that would have been annoying to Daddy at the time but really funny to him later when he would tell us about it.

The Model A's duties were expanded to include pickups and deliveries when Daddy expanded the garage business to include the sale of Norge kitchen appliances and Zenith TV's (*see more on the Model A in the second paragraph of Chapter 10*).

The versatility of the Model A didn't stop with road calls and appliance deliveries.

For example, it played a big role while we were building the "Blockhouse". During this period Daddy fastened a pipe vise at the rear of the truck bed. The pipe vise and attending flat wooden bed served as a workbench for threading all the galvanized pipe used in the plumbing of the house.

Also, since the old school property, on which the "Blockhouse" was built, already had sewer lines in the ground we were able to use some sections for our own system. However, some of the lines were excess and had to be removed. On one particular occasion, I remember that this entailed digging up at least one very long section of sewer pipe which was 6" in diameter. Once the dirt was removed the next problem was removing the extremely heavy cast-iron pipe from the trench. Since Daddy had no crane available, or 50 strong men standing around, he improvised. The Model A was positioned so that it straddled the open trench. Somehow Daddy was able to raise one end of the heavy sewer line up enough so that a chain could be placed under it and secured around the front axle of the Model A. He then climbed into the cab of the Model A and started it up. The little truck with its tiny 40 horsepower engine struggled but it pulled the heavy line out of the trench. My last memory of this is of the Model A driving away with the sewer line sliding along the ground between its four wheels.

During the time we had our Model A many of the roads in Mt. Juliet were unpaved. They were muddy when it rained and extremely dusty when it was dry...I'm not sure which problem was worse. On the one hand, muddy roads were the enemy of a car's underbelly—that is the abrasive grit from the muddy water caused a car's suspension and steering system to wear out prematurely. On the other hand, dusty roads made everyone suffer each time a car sped by and left a cloud of dust that would drift through the open windows of our then non-airconditioned homes, settle on the wash hanging on the line or be inhaled. Of the two I guess dust was disliked the most.

One way we fought the dust problem was with used motor oil.

Each time a customer came in for an oil change we drained about five quarts of oil from the engine's crankcase. Used oil wasn't recycled back then so there was always a plentiful supply stored in 30-gallon barrels out back of Castleman's Garage.

When we lived at the "Blockhouse" our neighbors and the Model A helped us spread used oil all along Second Avenue to give our homes a respite from the dust. A "V" shaped trough was made from galvanized metal and hundreds of small holes were drilled in the bottom of the "V". The trough was then mounted at the back edge of the Model A's stake bed. Next several of the barrels of used oil would be loaded on the back of the truck. The final step was to slowly drive the Model A up and down Second Avenue while a couple of strong helpers would pour oil in the "V" shaped trough. The oil would pass through the makeshift sieve and hit the ground. A lot of effort would yield only a short reprieve from a problem that would never be fixed until the road was finally paved more than a decade later.

Another story about the Model A involved learning to drive. I began learning when I was about 9 or 10. I could barley see over the steering wheel so I would pull myself up higher by clenching the steering wheel at 12:00 o'clock with both hands. Daddy caught me doing this and told me to get a cushion to sit on so I wouldn't need to do that. He then told me about the minor accident Richard had while using the same 12:00 o'clock grip method when he was me about my age and size. Richard and Daddy were in the Model A heading north on Mt. Juliet Road. Richard was driving and as they were rounding the slight curve in front of Rollie Peek's home (now the Mt. Juliet Post Office) the truck started veering from left to right. Because of Richard's physical size and the way, he was hanging on to the steering wheel he lost control. The truck ran off the road and knocked down a telephone pole before it stopped. No one was hurt and there was only minor damage to the Model A. Daddy said he contacted Walter Phillips, then owner of the Mt. Juliet Telephone Company, and the pole was replaced with little or no fanfare.

I had my own close shave with the Model A…

I was about five and we were still living in our garage home. It seemed like Richard, Daddy and I had been in and out of the truck all day for a variety of road calls and other short trips. All day long it had been Daddy at the wheel, Richard at "shotgun" and me in the middle straddling the floor mounted gearshift and handbrake. Because of my short height the only view I had was of the small simple instrument cluster located in the middle of the Model A's dash. Now I knew I was too young to be behind the wheel, but I saw no reason why Richard couldn't trade places with me and sit in the middle every now and then. Each time we got into the truck that day Richard and I had the same argument about who would ride next to the door. Daddy stayed out of the discussion. I guess he figured he'd let the two of us work it out.

Finally, it was time to close the garage for the day and head home for supper. The three of us headed for the truck for the two-block trip between the shop and our garage home. Once again, I complained about the seating arrangements in the truck and this time Richard finally gave in and let me ride there. The three of us had hardly gotten seated when Daddy roared away from the shop. About 20 feet into the trip and at a speed of about 10 miles an hour I was out the door. The rolled-up cuff on the left leg of my jeans caught on the running board and I was dragged on my head for about 10 feet before Daddy stopped.

I remember crying all the way home and long after until I was placed in the middle of Mother and Daddy's bed where I spent the night. I still have scares on the back of my head that could be seen if I wore a GI Haircut.

Although I often kidded Richard about pushing me out the door that day, I am sure he didn't (well, pretty sure). The body of that old Model A was in pretty bad condition and the door didn't fit against the body like it should. Also, there was actually no handle or latch on that door to keep it closed. A short time later Mother pointed out to me that Daddy had installed a screen door hook and eye on the inside of the door to keep it closed.

The old Model A was the first in a line of other faithful truck soldiers that helped support the family business. It would be followed by the purchase of a previously wrecked 1946 International pickup and a greatly abused 1948 Ford Pickup. All of these trucks were kept on life support by my Dad. They were old and battered but they earned their keep!

The old metaphor "the cobbler's children have no shoes" makes me think of a companion, "the auto mechanic drives old worn-out trucks and cars".

The front half of our 1928/29 Model A Ford truck. A close look reveals the original spoke wheels have been replaced with later model disk wheels; a piece of 4 by 8 lumber has replaced the standard Model A bumper in order to minimize damage to stalled autos being pushed back to life; the gas tank was right in front of the passenger compartment and the gas cap can be seen in the middle of the cowling just outside the windshield; the single windshield wiper was suspended at the top of the windshield and was operated back and forth by the driver. There were no cell phones then so the driver had a free hand to steer and operate the wiper with his other hand.

This is the best full shot of the Model A available. Here you can see a good portion of the stake bed. The lack of contour on the back of the truck's cab provides further evidence of modification from sedan to truck.

Left to right: standing is Jean (Bates) Conaster, Bettye, Jimmy Locke, Carolyn (Hunter) Swain; seated; me and Janice. The occasion was Bettye's 7th birthday party (April 10, 1950) when she was in the first grade. Jean, Jimmy and Carolyn were Bettye's honored guests from outside the family. Bettye remembers that she invited her classmates to her party, but that Mother didn't know about it until that day. Mrs. Ruth Gifford, first grade teacher for all five of us Castlemans, got wind of it and called Bettye into the coatroom to ask her about all the people she had invited. She then got in touch with Mother and as usual Mother came through and saved the day. It was a surprise birthday party but only to Mother.

CHAPTER **13**

Mother and Ladies Night at The Men's Club

IT WAS A Tuesday in mid-June of 1952 and the laborious task of mowing the two-acre lawn around the large concrete blockhouse had been finally finished the previous evening. The lush, rolling landscape would be inviting to the expected guests.

Several make-shift tables had been erected from assorted building supplies and because it was the evening meal, temporary lighting consisting of bare light bulbs dangling from heavy electric wiring, had been stretched from the roof of the house, over the tables and attached to trees or whatever was vertically available.

It was four o'clock, less than three hours before supper – Janice, Bettye and Evalena began carefully spreading white linen or oil-cloth tablecloths on the crude tables. Various species of silverware abounded that were neatly arranged to receive the eventual dinner plate filled with food.

Next came the chairs. Daddy's pickup truck, which was normally used for service calls at Castleman's Garage, was chartered to move fifty wooden folding chairs from the garage of the "Dude" Hibbet home (two doors away) to our front yard, where they would be unloaded, unfolded and set underneath the tables. "Dude" Hibbett was our local undertaker and part owner of a funeral home. Each folding chair had the name "McMillen and Hibbett" stenciled on its back and had been used at many a graveside.

By the time this was done, a mixture of smells from the evening meal began to move from the kitchen out into the yard. The trained nose of any of our family members could unscramble those aromas and mentally list only a part of the evening's menu:

Fried Chicken
Creamed Potatoes
Brewed Tea (for Iced Tea of course)
Homemade Yeast Rolls

Sometime during the afternoon two twenty-five-pound blocks of ice had been procured from McCorkle's Frozen Food Locker. One of us had the fun assignment of using an ice pick to chip the large blocks into hundreds of pieces small enough for iced tea glasses.

Mother had things organized and on schedule to serve supper to the Mt. Juliet Men's Civic Club. Tonight was special - it was "Ladies' Night".

Since Daddy was an active member of the club, all the supper's preparation and serving had to follow a rigid schedule so she could hopefully join him at his table for a few minutes, if not during the meal, then at least shortly after for part of the meeting.

The food didn't have an institutional or cafeteria taste – it was exceptionally good and Mother's reputation for excellence in the kitchen was well known. I'm convinced many of the men were members of the club, not because of a quest for civic involvement but because Katie's weekly Tuesday night meal was a treat. At 75 cents per plate, the price was right too. With a profit of 25 cents per plate, "Ladies Night" brought in $10-$12 of extra earnings for the family per week.

The ladies at "Ladies Night" didn't feel threatened by Katie's expertise and weren't afraid to compliment her. There were always comments like, "Katie, it's so good – I don't know how you do it!" Frankly, they probably couldn't have.

The ladies had to appreciate their husband's affection for Mother's cooking – after all it was undeniably good and tonight it was their night out of the kitchen.

I wrote this story as a Christmas present for Mother and gave it to her December 25, 1979.

No photo is available for the story on that night in 1952 so I came up with a good alternative. This 1948 photo made in the Mt. Juliet Elementary School Auditorium is a different kind of Ladies Night. Most of the members of the Mt. Juliet Men's Club are dressed up as women for a beauty pageant fundraiser to purchase lights for the new high school football field. The men played to a packed house and the fundraiser was a huge success. Funny thing, my Dad chose to laugh with the audience, and you can see the back of his head lower right in the photo.

Mt. Juliet High's first ever night time football game was played on a lighted field on September 17, 1948 between the Mt. Juliet Bears and Cumberland High School. Photo courtesy of Charles "Hooty" Smith..

CHAPTER 14

Napoleon Bonaparte

IF YOU LOOK closely at the ground just below the vertical Mohawk Tire sign in the photo above, you can barely see our full-blooded Cocker Spaniel, Napoleon Bonaparte. "Nappy", as we called him, was Castleman's Garage official mascot and a Mt. Juliet icon for about 12 years (1949-1962). He spent most of his life at the garage or the "Blockhouse".

Nappy loved to ride in our service truck with his head out the passenger door window…ears flying like Dumbo's.

He loved to run through the cornfield below the Blockhouse and in the fall his big ears would get so full of cockleburs that they would flop up as he ran until they would finally attach to each other in the up position. If I'd only been paying attention to this, I could have invented Velcro!

Like many dogs around Mt. Juliet during that time, he became a victim of intentional poisoning on at least two occasions. While I have no firsthand knowledge of this, I remember being told hot dogs laced with poison were used to bait unsuspecting dogs (animal cruelty is nothing new). Richard saved Nappy's life each time by rushing to the grocery to buy a can of lard. He would force the lard down Nappy's throat, Nappy would gag and the poison and everything else in Nappy's stomach would come up. Richard used to say the whole family claimed Nappy when all was well, but that he was only Richard's dog when he was sick.

Another cruel joke was played on Nappy that he never got over. At some point firecrackers were thrown at him at awfully close range (not by anyone in our family). This made him deathly afraid of loud noises. When it thundered or when the Tennessee Central Railroad Train would come by, Nappy would cower under the metal workbench inside Castleman's Garage until it was over.

Most people didn't bathe their dog back then and we were no exception. Nappy's collection of grease and dirt from his days at the garage were bad enough, but the cockleburs in his ears made it even worse. Nappy only had one or two baths in his life. On one of these rare occasions someone in the family took this circa 1961 photo below while Bettye and I struggled with what is obviously a very unhappy subject.

Nappy helped make our family complete and will never be forgotten.

Below, Janice holds Nappy as a pup. (photo circa 1950)

CHAPTER 15

How I Love To Drive My Buick

ON SATURDAY NIGHTS during 1959 and 1960 I made many 15 mile motorcycle trips to Martin Motors on highway 231 south of Lebanon, Tennessee (near Bairds Mill). There I'd meet up with my friend, A.D. "Junior" Martin, and we'd hang out. His Dad's place of business was known as "the station" to us.

"Dud", Junior's Dad, was the owner and was usually there. He sold new and used cars, gasoline and junk car parts. He had over a thousand junk cars so people were always there pulling used parts to fix their cars. This large "we never close" operation sprawled over several acres on each side of the highway.

Hanging out at the station often included playing the juke box, riding around in one of the many cars, going to Lebanon to get a burger, throwing eggs at cars along the highway or even a short road trip to Kentucky.

On one particular Saturday night in June of 1960, Junior showed me a gently used 1957 Buick Roadmaster that his Dad had just gotten in. I'm pretty sure we went for a ride in it and I thought it was a beautiful, truly luxurious car. It was a two-toned blue, 4 door hard-top, with air conditioning, electric windows and power everything. The next morning I raved about the car to Daddy over Sunday breakfast and encouraged him to go take a look at it. To my surprise he said let's go after church.

Since Daddy owned and operated Castleman's Garage and could repair anything, we'd always driven pretty old cars. The family car at

that time was a 10 year old 1950 Oldsmobile. So I was shocked that
after our visit to see the '57 Roadmaster he decided to buy it from
Dud! Wow, a family car only three years old! It became the newest and
nicest car our family had ever owned.

The very first time I was allowed to drive it solo was between
Castleman's Garage and the Blockhouse, all of 2 blocks away. I got
behind the wheel, hit the buttons to adjust the electric seat and roll
up the electric windows. I then turned on the air conditioner and AM
radio. About 500 hundred feet from the large shade tree where I was
to park at the Blockhouse, one of the greatest car advertising songs of
all time began playing on the radio...

"How I love to drive my Buick
With my love sitting by my side;
Pretty girl and shiny Buick
Fills a fella with so much pride.
Driving down the road on Sunday
with my car and my heart riding high,
For I know that very soon
We'll take a honeymoon,
My Buick, my love, and I."

All this had to be divine intervention I thought. It was a song I loved and I still know some of the lyrics. I'd first heard it in the early 50's when Buick became a sponsor on the Milton Berle TV Show. I was truly in hog heaven for the next 30 minutes sitting in a luxury automobile, parked under that shade tree, and listening to the radio in an air-conditioned automobile!

Our '57 Buick Roadmaster, two-toned blue, 4 Door Hardtop c.1960

And so, I became smitten with Buicks for a while...

Then there was my own Buick story...

Sometime around 1961 I was hunting down used car parts for Daddy in a junkyard located on US 70 between Mt. Juliet and Lebanon. It was there I found a '55 Buick Century, two-door hardtop, up on blocks with no wheels. It had a good engine, a bad automatic "Dynaflow" transmission, and the lower quarter panels on the rear fenders were rusted out. The junk yard owners had the intention of "parting-it-out".

I went back to the garage and talked Daddy into going with me to take a look at it. We checked it over and he agreed to fix the automatic transmission and show me how to patch and paint the rusted out portion of the rear fenders. We negotiated a price of $400. The next step was to put wheels on the car and tow it home.

We headed back to the garage with four empty Buick wheel rims and I found four very slick tube-type tires in our junk pile to mount on them. Later we headed back to the junk yard, put the car on the ground with wheels and towed it back to the garage behind our '48 Ford service truck.

The transmission repair was the first order of business. It had to be removed from the car and that was a nightmare. The '55 had an enclosed drive shaft so it was necessary to unbolt the entire rear drive train from the body of the car and then roll the complete rear wheel suspension system toward the rear of the jacked up car body. Only then could the transmission be removed.

At that time (and as I mentioned in Chapter 2), Daddy was teaching himself how to repair automatic transmissions. The intricacies of automatic transmissions were then and still is mind boggling. Only someone with his ability and patience could master a rebuild without going to school. My Buick gave him another project on which to learn.

Unfortunately my rough driving and drag racing at Union Hill Drag Strip were big contributing factors to the 2-3 additional times we had to take the transmission out and repair it all over again. He never became the least bit discouraged. Although it was never discussed, I think he was well aware of my antics and wanted to prove his work could stand up to an abusive teenage driver. He soon became a master of the self-taught skill of automatic transmission repair.

My '55 Buick Century 2 door hardtop in blue in and white. This was soon after I rescued it from the junk yard and a rebuilt transmission got it going.

In between the chronic transmission rebuilds, we worked on re-pairing the rusted holes in the lower quarter panels of the rear fenders. A careful buyer in Tennessee in those days would avoid buying a car like this because it was most likely from a northern state where salt was used on snowy roads. But we knew about the rust issues going in and were prepared to tackle the problem.

Some of the holes were so large you could stick your hand through them. After grinding and sanding all the rust away Daddy came up with the idea of cutting screen wire the size of the hole and then tack welding it in place. The screen wire then provided a backing to hold the Bondo body filler in place. Bondo was, and probably still is, a mix-ture of goop that contains, among other things, fiberglass (polyester) resin, talc and a hardening agent. The Bondo was then quickly applied to the car with a putty knife and shaped to the contour of the car be-fore it became hard and stable. It would begin to set, hard as a rock, within a few minutes aided by our floor mounted work light which was used on the area to add heat to the Bondo curing process. It all seemed to take only a few minutes. Then lots of power grinding and hand sanding were needed next to shape the Bondo to the true form of the fender. Tons of toxic dust emanated from all this work that nowadays would only be done with protective masks and clothing.

Examples of how the rust looked on the left and after Bondo on the right.

After spraying a prime coat on the area, we applied a finishing coat of paint that had been matched with the Buick's original factory paint number. It turned out great!

One other adventure involving the '55 happened late one cold Saturday night in 1961 while returning home from a date in Gladeville, TN. I was driving north toward Mt. Juliet, on what was then the unpaved portion of South Mt. Juliet Road. To add insult to injury the road crossed Suggs Creek via a one lane metal bridge with loose wood planks for flooring. You heard the sound of loose planks against metal as you crossed and never quite dismissed the idea that the bridge was going down and taking you with it.

The road on both ends was lower than the bridge itself, even lower on the south end. It could be deceptive to motorists because the road on the south side of the bridge could be 3-4 feet under water while the bridge was yet to be flooded. It was not uncommon for a car to stall in this area with a flooded-out engine.

The north side was particularly rough since it was made up of uneven, very large and somewhat flat natural limestone rocks that joined each other very unevenly. These rocks were so large they could only have been moved with dynamite. There was an attempt to smooth out that part of the road a bit with gravel but the big rocks ruled.

On several prior occasions I had driven across in axle deep water. During heavy rains the creek crossing was impassable.

My first memory of crossing Suggs Creek there was around 1953 or 1954. I don't know why we were over that way, but my older brother Richard was driving our old International pickup and we were heading toward Mt. Juliet. He always had the radio on. Just as we got to the south side of the bridge the radio station started playing Andy Griffith's "What it was, was football". To this day, anytime I hear that recording I remember crossing that old bridge.

Several years later our school secretary, Mary Patton, stalled her Dodge in standing water as she was crossing the bridge. She got out of the car okay and Daddy was somehow summoned for road service help. By the time he arrived the water was getting deeper and deeper. Daddy said there was a crowd of male on-lookers who had all attempted to help but failed. Finally, he removed his pants and waded to the car with a log chain. After hooking it to the car's bumper and then the back of his truck he pulled the car out. I'm still amazed that during those times he did all this in his boxer shorts in front of Mary Patton and even the male audience. I am even more amazed at how nonchalantly he told me about it.

Okay so I digressed a bit but you get the picture.

Luckily on this night the creek was down. But it was at this lovely spot, and just a few feet from crossing the rickety bridge, that my Buick decided to begin making a terrible engine noise and missing badly. I was forced to stop and pull as far off the narrow road as possible so I wouldn't block the one lane bridge.

It was now around 11:00pm. I put on my coat for a cold walk south on the dark country road back to Stewarts Ferry Pike. From there I headed east toward Gladeville to the nearest house I remembered seeing. It was my first time to knock on the door of an old dark farmhouse with nothing else around. Back then I wasn't afraid of rousing someone I didn't know to ask for help. An old man came to the door and I introduced myself as Macon Castleman's boy. He of course knew who my Dad was and let me use his phone to call. (The Mt. Juliet Telephone Company had not yet converted to dial phones).

"881-W" I told the telephone operator and I soon began hearing the phone ringing at my home. Daddy sleepily answered the phone and I briefly told him where the car was located. Without hesitation he said he was on his way. I left the old man's house and walked roughly a mile back to the car to wait.

Within 30 minutes Daddy arrived in our old '48 Ford pickup service truck. We couldn't push or tow the car back home since that would ruin the automatic transmission. So with no complaints about the late hour, he helped me remove one of the valve covers and determine a valve rocker arm had broken away on one of the eight cylinders. All this was done with tools we always carried with us and with the aid of a flashlight.

Since there was too much damage to repair on the roadside he quickly came up with the idea of temporarily repositioning the rocker arm and removing the spark plug wire to that cylinder. That disabled the firing of that cylinder and enabled the engine to run a little more smoothly and less noisily.

I drove home on 7 of the 8 cylinders at a slow speed. It was well past midnight by the time we reached home but there was no lecture from Daddy about rescuing me well after his normal bedtime.

And in keeping with the late hour regarding the above event, I should go on record to say the work we did on my car or any of the family cars was done after hours or in between all the other work going on at Castleman's Garage. No customer work was delayed or deferred because of work on our cars.

Our faithful old 1948 Ford service truck. It pushed and pulled cars (with a log chain) on hundreds of road calls. The log chain, a booster battery, a can of gas, a few tools, a jack and lug wrench were always carried in the truck bed.

My '55 with most of the body work done and factory hubcaps replaced with "Spinners".

Daddy wasn't a demonstrative man until late in life. But he showed his love in those years in many other ways. He was very supportive of all my automobile projects. He wanted to pass along his knowledge to me and did it in a very kind and patient way. Even after I was grown and moved away I would call him for advice and help on my auto repairs.

I could handle more routine work like brake overhauls, tune-ups and normal maintenance, but bigger projects gave me an opportunity to ask him for help. We both enjoyed these phone conversations.

While I was living in Los Angeles for 5 1/2 years in the early 70s he talked me through a valve job on my Toyota. While living near New York City for 3 years in the late 70s, I had to replace the engine in my Chevrolet Vega with a used engine from a wrecked Vega I located in a Brooklyn junk yard. I phoned him for guidance on numerous occasions on that project and have him to thank for making it a success.

After moving to the DFW area in 1980s I became a little more self sufficient. In the mid 90s, after he'd passed away, I successfully replaced a bad cylinder head on my son Joe's Chrysler Laser. Even then he was there for me in spirit.

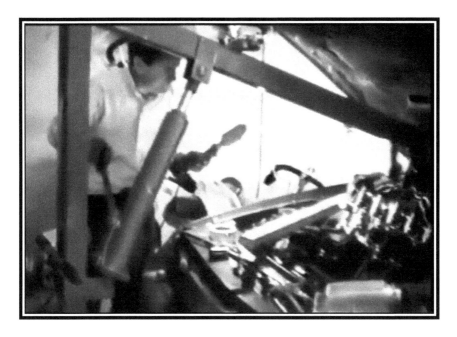

Me replacing the cylinder head on my son Joe's Chrysler Laser around 1995.

I had a different kind of career from my Dad and never became a master mechanic, but I got by. Daddy's generous mentoring and great teaching skills enabled me to do all my own auto repairs for a good part of my life. It wasn't until I was in my early 50s that I finally began to pay someone else to do my auto work.

I'm blessed that most of his shop tools were handed down to me. Every now and then I still putter a bit with cars in my home garage.

I remain my Dad's humble apprentice!

This black and white version of a color painting was done for me by my sister Evalena. The original hangs in my home office as a daily reminder of the happy times of my beginnings!

Epilogue

ONE QUESTION SOME may ask about this book is why did I dwell so much on a particular window of time? Roughly speaking, 1948 through 1961—or ages 4 through 16 for me.

Writing this book about that particular time period has helped bring me some inner peace. And, it has helped me learn things about this early part of my life that I didn't know at the time.

Some examples…

Little did I know that those years of my early life were when the foundation of my life was being created.

Little did I know what an influence those years would have throughout my life.

Little did I know the life skills I learned growing up in the family business would become priceless career skills.

Little did I know how much I would value the goodness of the people of Mt. Juliet—both related and unrelated.

Little did I know then how fortunate I was to be growing up in an extraordinary town during an extraordinary time.

Little did I know how lucky I was to have been born into an extraordinary family…complete with all the trimmings…a wonderful Mother and Father, a wonderful brother and three wonderful sisters.

And little did I know how all these things would help me to marry well and have three wonderful children!

Acknowledgements

MY FAMILY AND friends have been an ongoing inspiration to me in completing this work. To all of you, I say thank you!

I am grateful to John Crosby who was briefly a teacher in my 8th grade year. His powerful enthusiasm and mentoring style from back then and again most recently has helped me to finally move my manuscript to publication.

Also, I greatly appreciate John Crosby for introducing me to my newest friend, George Rothacker, who did a superb job of designing the book cover.

I'm beholden to my life-long friend Charles Lee McCorkle who always encouraged me, helped with Mt. Juliet history, did proof reading and then wrote a beautiful introduction which captures the essence of the book.

And I'm especially thankful to my wife Diane for always being there and helping me over the years by proofreading and suggesting better ways to present my thoughts.

As we used to say in Mt. Juliet, I'm much obliged!

About the Author

Ron Castleman began working at the age of 10 at his father's auto repair business in Mt. Juliet, Tennessee. Since graduating from Middle Tennessee State University he held senior level management positions for both large and small corporations in major U.S. cities. Yet he has never lost touch with childhood friends and continues to highly value growing up in a small rural community.

Following a successful corporate career, Ron served as Chief Operating Officer of the Federal Emergency Management Agency (FEMA). At FEMA he was responsible for the day-to-day agency operation of response, recovery, preparedness and national security coordination activities for the United States and its territories. Also, while at FEMA he served as the head of the U.S. Civil Emergency Planning Delegation to NATO in Brussels where he addressed all Allied Nations in the NATO Council Chamber.

In 2007 he launched WRC Associates, an independent homeland security consulting business. He continues to serve federal clients in Washington, DC

Ron has been married to Diane since his college years and they have three grown children and six grandchildren. He lives in Texas, but *"Julip"* will always be home!

Lightning Source UK Ltd.
Milton Keynes UK
UKHW020007281221
396261UK00010B/340/J